F My Life

F My Life

Maxime Valette,
Guillaume Passaglia,
& Didier Guedj

Illustrations by
Marie "Missbean" Levesque

VILLARD Ⓥ NEW YORK

Published in the United States by Villard Books, an imprint of
The Random House Publishing Group, a division of Random House, Inc., New York.

VILLARD BOOKS and VILLARD & "V" CIRCLED Design are registered trademarks of
Random House, Inc.

Some material originally published in France by Michel Lafon in 2008.

This edition published through and by arrangement with Michel Lafon Publishings.

Library of Congress Cataloging-in-Publication Data

Valette, Maxime
F my life / Maxime Valette, Guillaume Passaglia & Didier Guedj; illustrations by
Marie "Missbean" Levesque.
p. cm.
ISBN 978-0-345-51876-7 (pbk.)
1. Conduct of life—Humor.   2. Embarrassment—Humor.
I. Passaglia, Guillaume, 1982–   II. Guedj, Didier.   III. Title.
PN6231.C6142V35 2009
818'.60208—dc22   2009015163

Printed in the United States of America

www.villard.com

246897531

Book design by Susan Turner

Contents

A Short History of FML

It all started in a chat room. A few buddies in France got into the habit of telling each other the crappy things that had happened to them that day—what made their day completely suck. The forum then became a blog in January 2008, and we named it Vie de Merde ("Shitty Life"). As interest in these stories began to reach a wider audience, the website grew and grew, and we just knew we had to welcome the entire English language aboard our mission. Fmylife.com soon had visitors from all around the globe. Quickly we realized something *very* interesting: that the same kind of shitty events occur all over the world, every day, to all sorts of people. There is a kind of solidarity among all countries when it comes to misfortune. We are all in a big, international pile of crap. We are in it together, the one sad worldwide universality in life.

We can definitely say that it is all Maxime's fault. He started all this by messing around on the Web, coming up with the concept and then the French website. Guillaume later joined him to help out, and after a while they asked Didier to take part in the F My Life adventure. This is how the whole thing started and continues to carry on.

We'd like to thank the literally thousands and thousands of people who had the requisite sense of humor and self-deprecation to send us their tales of troubles and strife. It's become a gold mine of crap and embarrassment, and it's amazing. But working in a mine, you have to push that little bit harder to extract the real gems, which is now our full-time job. Of course, the joy of finding a new story that makes us smile or laugh is still fresh for all of us. This is gold, people! Keep it up!

Enjoy!

F My Life

Moments of Shame

Embarrassment, rejection, getting unceremoniously
dumped—some of us are used to such occurrences
by now and have nearly turned them into a new art
form. In small doses, shame can be a good thing;
it teaches us to be humble and provides an instant
cure for arrogance. If those who have survived the
worst are able to tell their story, it means they're
still standing. (Sort of.) Which just goes to show
that self-mockery might be one of the world's most
useful survival instincts. . . .

Today, thinking I was being very generous, I lent my jacket to my new co-worker. Maybe I should have checked my pockets first. I'm not sure that having three different flavors of condoms made a good impression. FML

Today I was at work at the grocery store, and a woman pulled a cart toward me filled with chips, breads, lunch meats, and sodas. I said to her, "Looks like you're going to have a fun party!" She looked back at me and said, "My mother just died. This is for after the funeral." FML

Today I ate at a friend's house. When she left the table for a few minutes, her five-year-old son looked at me and said quietly, "You're ugly!" When my friend came back, I told her what had happened. She scolded him briefly, and then the boy began to cry, shouting, "But she isn't pretty!" FML

Today my boyfriend was lying on top of me and looking at me with passion in his eyes. I thought he was finally going to tell me he loved me. But instead he said, "You have a booger." FML

Today I'm in Spain. In Spanish, I told my students that I was excited to be working with them. However, the form of the word for "excitement" that I used apparently refers to sexual excitement. So I actually told the kids I was sexually aroused to be working with them. FML

Today while I was out having a drink with a pretty girl, she looked at my crotch and said with a smile, "There's something burning down there." I smiled back, but she was insistent. Cigarette ashes had set my trousers on fire. FML

Today when I woke up, my husband was already out of bed. Thinking I was hearing him padding by in the hall, I shouted, "Get that cock in here right now!" A voice replied, "He's gone out to get some bread." It was my mother-in-law. FML

Today I put my hand up in class. I forgot that I hadn't shaved my armpits. FML

Today a child sitting next to me
on the bus pointed at me and asked,
"Mommy, if it's not a man and it's
not a woman, what is it then?" FML

Today I had a job interview at a restaurant that was opening up. One manager asked me why I should be hired. I said I was more efficient than most people. When the interview was over, I left to find that I'd locked my keys in the car. It took all the managers to help me get my keys out. FML

Today I decided to practice putting a condom on with my mouth. My roommate walked in on me while I was using my mouth to roll a condom onto a banana. FML

Today I had the first meeting with my new bosses. We went to a restaurant for lunch. I choked on a piece of meat and couldn't breathe. I had to take that piece of meat out of my throat with my fingers and then put it back on my plate all chewed up. FML

Today I played in a tennis tournament. After winning, I went to shake my opponent's hand. He didn't react or move. It was only the first set. FML

Today I was walking through Borders bookstore with my girl-friend when we passed a stand selling Girl Scout cookies. I saw a box of Samoas, my favorite, so I pointed to them and shouted, "YEAH!" My girlfriend looked shocked. Behind the box of cookies was a nine-year-old scout bending over, with her bottom pointed at me. FML

Today I had an important appointment for a potential job. During the interview, my cell phone rang. My ringtone is the theme song from *Inspector Gadget*. FML

Today I made love to my girlfriend. I penetrated her for a while, then stopped to get my breath back. She carried on moaning, even though I'd stopped moving. FML

Today I went to a plastic surgeon's
office with a friend. The doctor
walked in, and before he could look
at the chart, he started explaining
the liposuction procedure to me.
I had to interrupt him to tell him
that I was only there to support
my friend who was getting a nose
job. FML

Today I dressed in my sexiest clothes (Gucci and Prada, worth a real fortune) to meet my new boyfriend at a restaurant. As I was a bit early, I took the opportunity to smoke a cigarette outside in front of the door while I was waiting. The restaurant owner came out and said, "Hey, you! Go and 'work' somewhere else, please." FML

Today, to amuse my girlfriend, I put on her sexy nightshirt and went out on the balcony for a smoke, wriggling about in front of her window. She laughed, until one of her neighbors shouted "Hello!" from the upper floor, grinning at the show. FML

Today, at a rehearsal, a friend poked me and said, "My mother is in the orchestra. Guess who she is!" I jokingly answered, "Umm...the fat singer?" It was. FML

Today, in the supermarket, everybody was staring at me. After ten minutes, I realized that my umbrella was still open. FML

Today my wife and I went to a wedding. At 1:00 in the morning (when the cake was being served), we were starting to fall asleep at the table, so we went to our car to take a short nap. When we woke up, at about 5:00, the party was over. FML

Today it's been two weeks since I lost my virginity, and I've already had sex with three guys. FML

Today I received a really nice set of red satin underwear, with a bra, a thong, and a corset . . . from my grandfather. FML

Today I fell asleep on the train, totally wiped out after the previous night's party, which featured lots of booze and very spicy Indian food. I woke up and noticed a small boy in the seat in front of me staring back at me. I smiled at him, and then he turned to his father and said, "Daddy, the farting man just woke up." FML

Today, as a med student in my sixth year, I spent the whole day in surgery. No one told me that what I was wearing on my feet was actually supposed to be put over my hair. FML

Today my watch broke, so I mentioned to my dad that I needed a new one. A bit later he handed me a really nice watch. He said, "Here, this one's been lying around for a while." It was his Father's Day present. FML

Today a co-worker and I walked out of our office at the same time. He got into his car, which was parked right out front. I asked him what I had to do to get a sweet parking spot like that. He proceeded to roll up his pant leg and show me his prosthesis. He was in the handicapped spot. FML

Today I thought I was going on a date. About twenty minutes into it, like a true gentleman, I gave her my arm to hold. It came up in conversation that my brother is gay. Her response: "Oh, so both you and your brother are gay?" FML

Today my boyfriend and I were looking for our bubble-gum-flavored numbing lotion to have some morning fun. We couldn't find it anywhere. After about ten minutes, my little nephew walked out of my room crying, with drool coming out of his mouth. He smelled like bubble gum, and his mouth and tongue were numb. FML

Today, as I came out of a store dressing room, I gave all the stuff I'd tried on to a saleswoman. Then I walked off, making it a couple of steps before I changed my mind and decided to purchase one of the items. When I got back, the saleswoman was spraying the changing room I'd used with deodorant. FML

Today, while on a date with the guy of my dreams, I cut my tongue so badly it bled for an hour. I had cut it on the plastic spoon from my coffee. FML

Today I got together at a bar with a small group of friends. I went to order a drink, but with all the music and noise, the bartender couldn't hear what I was trying to say, so he leaned forward, cocking his ear toward me. I thought he was being very friendly, so I kissed him. FML

Today I was at an interview for a
music school. When I got my guitar
out of its case, I realized that my
friends had thought it would be funny
to replace my real guitar with one
from the Guitar Hero video game. FML

Today I went home for my grandma's ninety-fifth birthday. When I
got there, she noticed my new tongue piercing and asked why I
would get that done. Before I could reply, my cousin said, "So she
can make the boys happier when she's sucking on them." She's
nine years old. FML

Today I had to give a speech about fire safety onstage at a local
preschool. I'm thirty-two years old, and I passed out on the
stage because I was intimidated by a group of four-year-olds.
FML

Today I was sitting on the couch, computer next to me, lotion
on the floor, and my dick in my hand, when my roommate
walked in. Looking me right in the face with a scared expres-
sion, he said, "What's for dinner?" FML

Today in class I asked my teacher for a rubber. I didn't realize that in America "rubber" doesn't mean "eraser," it means "condom." FML

Today, since I am an exchange student in Mexico, someone asked me what it's like to be from Minnesota. I responded in Spanish, in front of thirty people, saying what I thought translated to "If you get cold, you can just put on a jacket." Apparently, what I actually said meant "If you get cold, you can just masturbate." FML

Today I sang the itsy-bitsy spider song with a class of thirty twenty-somethings because we're going to be kindergarten teachers. The teacher made us do the hand motions, too. FML

Today three girls introduced themselves to me. I had met all of them before. FML

Today I was eating at a restaurant
with my boyfriend. He is six foot
two, and I'm four foot eleven. Out
of nowhere, the hostess started
openly flirting with him and asked
him if he needed a high chair for
his daughter. FML

missbean

Today I went to the gym to try to get into shape. I pulled a muscle while taking off my sweater in the locker room. FML

Today my nephew asked me how babies are made. I thought he'd had this chat with his mom, but I went into it again. After a twenty-minute "discussion," he said, "So what about the good stuff? Get to the blow jobs and the lesbians." He's eleven. FML

Today my girlfriend caught me picking my nose and eating the booger. FML

Today my best friend was crying because her boyfriend is an idiot. I brought my thumb up to wipe a tear off her face and somehow stuck it up her nose. FML

Today my mother called to say that my eleven-year-old nephew found my secret stash of nipple tassels, furry handcuffs, and a bottle of lube. He doesn't want to visit me anymore. FML

Today I farted *a lot* during my exam, but it was all silently, so I figured I was okay. Then I looked around, and everybody was faking suffocation and giving me sly looks. I am now known to everyone in the department as Super Fart. FML

Today at work a man walked up the escalator with his chubby kid next to him and asked me where the shoe department was. I said, "For you or your son?" He replied, "For my daughter." FML

Today my anatomy teacher was putting together a skeleton model for class. He had misplaced the leg bone, so I thoughtfully asked, "What's the matter, lose a leg?" Unfortunately, there's nothing funny about asking that question of a guy who's had a leg amputated. FML

Today my friends and I went to a bar and proceeded to get wasted. I was walking around and saw a kid. I started yelling, "There's a child in this bar! There's a CHILD in this BAR!" She turned around. She was a little person. FML

Today I accidentally unplugged my headphones in the quiet section of the library, causing my music to play from my laptop at full volume. I was listening to Celine Dion. I'm the captain of the football team. FML

Today I finished having sex with my girlfriend, and she asked if I had started smoking weed again. I said yes and asked if she could smell it on me, since I had recently smoked. She replied, "The only time you can last this long is when you're high." FML

Today I was in the car with a group of my girlfriends, discussing sexual experiences. I looked down and realized that my BlackBerry had dialed the family I babysit for and left a five-minute voice mail. FML

Today my crush talked to me for the first time. He told me to stop staring. FML

Today my girlfriend of one month and I had an amazing night of dinner and dancing, but when I leaned in to kiss her, she said, "You're joking, right?" FML

Today I fell asleep in my driver's ed class, and I woke up in the middle of a dream, laughing. Everyone stared at me. I found out that the teacher had just finished talking about his niece who hadn't worn a seat belt and was now brain-dead. FML

Today I was instructed by my boss to welcome the two new foreign business partners because I am the only one who can speak their language. When they arrived, I greeted them in their language. One of them scratched his head and asked his companion in plain and clear English, "What did he say?" FML

Today I fell asleep in the train.
When I woke up, everybody was
staring at me with strange smiles
on their faces. I'll probably never
know what I did. FML

Today I was working the register at a
local grocery store. A kid about five
years old was having trouble zipping
his jacket. When I reached out to help
him, he started screaming, "No, bad
touch, bad touch!" and kicked me in
the knee. Everyone looked. FML

Today, when I threw my cigarette out of the car window, the
wind blew it back in again. My pants got completely burned.
FML

Today I was making love with my girlfriend, and my landline
rang. Obviously, I let it go to voice mail. At the very moment I
was about to climax, I heard my mom's voice on my machine:
"Hi, sweetheart." FML

Today I went out to dinner with my family. I was given a kids
menu when the hostess seated us. I'm twenty-four. FML

Today my four-year-old cousin gave me a hug, basically stuffing his face into my crotch. Then he pulled back and said, "Ew, that's stinky," in front of my entire class. FML

Today, while walking through the fragrance department in a department store, a women behind me said, "Excuse me, miss, would you like to sample our new fragrance line?" I'm a nineteen-year-old male. I turned around, expecting her to correct herself. She didn't. FML

Today, in the middle of a dinner date, I went to rest my chin on my hand, missed, and stuck the straw from my drink straight up my nose. My nose bled all over the table. He hasn't called me since. FML

Today at church, the little boy sitting behind me asked his mother if I had the chicken pox, because there were red dots all over my face. I've had bad acne since I was twelve. FML

Today I was talking to my crush about making the soccer team. Excited, he congratulated me and asked for my number. I proceeded to give him my cell phone number. He laughed and said, "Your jersey number." FML

Today, after I had filled up my car and got into it, I saw a cute guy running toward me. I flashed a smile and left the door open, saying "Hey" when he was next to me. He said, "The pump is still attached to your car—you really should be more careful." FML

Today I got a "save the date" card for the wedding of a couple my husband knows. I was excited because I really want to be better friends with these people. I emailed the bride, saying "I got your STD!" and hit Send before I realized how that sounded. FML

Today my group of friends, my girlfriend, and I were playing "Never have I ever." My girlfriend's turn came up, and she went with "Never have I ever had an orgasm." FML

Today I decided to brush up on my flirting skills and ask a guy I thought was kind of cute what time it was. He pointed to the very visible watch on my wrist and said, "You should know already." FML

Today my parents met my boyfriend's parents for the first time . . . bailing us out of jail. FML

Today my professor, who was born without arms, asked somebody, "Need a hand?" There are over three hundred students in that class, and I was the only one laughing. FML

Today, as I walked out of the bathroom, two guys were checking me out. One of them said, "Nice tail." I smiled and strutted to my next class. As I was about to sit down at my desk, the girl behind me said, "Did you know you have toilet paper hanging out of your pants?" FML

Today I was having sex with my girlfriend for the first time, and she asked me if I ever get made fun of in the locker room because of my small penis. FML

Today, I was DJing a wedding. The groom wanted me to play a song for his grandma and grandpa. I announced over the microphone that his grandparents should come to the dance floor for a special song. It turned out that his grandparents had been dead for over a year, and the song was supposed to be in dedication. FML

Today I was interviewing a cute guy for my journalism class, and he asked to borrow my laptop to check his email quickly. After the interview I realized that the last thing I had searched for with my browser was "ingrown pubic hairs"—and the words were still up there. FML

Today at a party I told this guy that I really liked his pirate costume. It turned out that he wasn't wearing a costume; his eye had been shot out with a BB gun. That explains the eye patch. FML

Today I drove to a job interview. I had to sneeze, but because I was driving on the highway I didn't let go of the wheel to cover my mouth. I didn't know the sneeze would be a "productive" one until I was sitting in the interview, looked down at my new blouse, and saw the giant loogie stuck there. FML

Today I went on the best date I've been on in years. Later, over drinks, we got to talking, and I explained how I came out to my friends and family. When I asked him how he came out, he replied that he isn't gay, and, oh, did I think this was a date? FML

Today I took the subway to school, and the man across from me would not stop staring at my breasts. Finally, the train came to my stop. As I got up, I said, "Nothing to see now, asshole." Then I noticed his white cane as he got up to get off, too. He was blind. FML

```
Today I went to get a haircut, and I
asked how much it was for a shampoo,
a haircut, and a blow job. I meant
to say "blow dry." FML
```

Today I went to a birthday party for
my friend's daughter. I picked up a
gift for the girl and another for
her parents. I got the mother a
cute little garden stone that read
"What our children see in the world
depends on what we show them." Later
I found out that her daughter is
blind. FML

Today I got a 31 percent on a Chinese test at school. I moved here to New Jersey from Beijing two months ago. FML

Today I was in Spanish class, having a debate about the death penalty. I was trying to make a point and I meant to say *"la pena de muerte,"* which means "the death penalty." Instead, I said, *"la pene de muerte."* It turns out that that means "the penis of death." FML

Today I was in my room and I drew a Harry Potter lightning bolt on my forehead in eyeliner, just because it cheers me up. Some friends dropped by casually, and we went out to get ice cream. When I got back, I realized the lightning bolt was still there. I'm in college. FML

Today I was typing up a love letter on my computer—a sexual love letter. I was in a classroom, I'm the teacher, I'm gay, and my love letter showed up on the TV screen while my seventh-grade students were taking a test. It was up on the screen for fifteen minutes. FML

Today I was meeting friends for dinner at an Indian restaurant. I was waiting for the group to arrive and our table to be ready. An Indian man approached me, smiling, so I said, "We're not ready for our table yet." Then I realized it was my friend's boyfriend, whom I've met several times. FML

Today I was sitting beside this cute guy on a bench. Suddenly he said, "I know we don't know each other very well, but would you like to have dinner on Saturday?" I turned to him with a goofy smile and exclaimed, "I'd *love* to!" He gave me a weird look, turned his head, and pointed to his Bluetooth. FML

Today my friend and I went to a tacky-themed party. She was wearing orange faux-snake stilettos. I commented, "Those are perfect for tonight. Where'd you manage to find such hideous shoes?" It turned out that she wears those shoes all the time--the color just matched her outfit. FML

Today I hit a parked car. I was walking. To make the scene more embarrassing, the car alarm shocked me, and I backed up quickly into the parking meter, which knocked me down. FML

Today I was driving on the freeway in the backseat of my friend's car. I looked over to the left and was greeted by a van full of adolescent boys waving and making the "call me" hand gesture. I then happened to looked down and realized that my right boob was completely out. FML

Today, in a very crowded public restroom at a sporting arena, after looking at the man using the urinal to his right, my six-year-old son turned to me and exclaimed, "Daddy, that man's wiener is a lot bigger than yours!" The whole bathroom heard. FML

Today, as I was getting restless in my psychology class, I proceeded to stretch out both of my arms and hands into the aisles on either side of me, only to find myself with my teacher's package in my palm. FML

Today I was pushing my four-year-old on the swing. I did what we call our "under doggie push": I push her up in the air while I run underneath her before she hits me coming back down. I walked away to get my water, and she yelled across the park, "Can we do it doggie-style again?" FML

Today I was alone in the break room at work when I got a slight pain in my belly. I thought I needed to pass gas, so I tried, since no one else was in there. It wasn't gas. It was diarrhea. I'm wearing a miniskirt today. FML

Today I was working at the grocery store, and a very old woman wanted to give me a tip for bagging her groceries. She slid a quarter into my pocket against my thigh as deep down as she could get it, then she gave me a smile and a wink. I was groped by a grandma. FML

Today I was babysitting an eleven-year-old boy. He decided we should play with Nerf guns that had Velcro tips. I accidentally shot him in the crotch, and the dart stuck on his pants, wiggling for about a full minute before his dad walked in to find us both staring at his son's crotch and giggling. FML

Today I was giving a friend a neck rub, when she started to breathe heavily. I figured she was getting into it, so I started kissing her neck. She turned around and said, "Tell my roommate I'm having an asthma attack." FML

Today I was teaching a swimming
lesson to six- and seven-year-old
boys and girls. I recently broke
up with my boyfriend, so I haven't
been taking care of my bikini line.
While I was demonstrating how to do
a whip-kick out of the water, one
of the boys said, "You have a beard
coming out of your bathing suit!"
FML

Today I decided to get dressed up for school because it's my birthday. I was heading to class in my heels. Then I turned my ankle, fell down a muddy hill, pulled a leg muscle, and scratched up my knees. At least ten people saw it. I was wearing a white skirt. Happy birthday. FML

Today, in front of twenty guests, I yelled at my spouse for not coming to blow out his birthday cake candles. It turned out that he was in the other room, quietly changing his disabled friend's adult diaper. FML

Today I was taking a shower after basketball practice. When I got out of the shower, I figured no one was home, so I thought it might be fun to walk around the house completely naked. I walked downstairs, and my mom was there eating dinner . . . along with twenty other members of her book club. FML

Today, on a ten-hour trip with my family, I fell asleep in the car as soon as we got on the highway. When I woke up an hour later, I realized I'd had a wet dream. I had to sit next to my grandma with semen all over my thighs and boxers for the rest of the trip. FML

Today my mom told my boyfriend all about how she had to be a parent volunteer when I was in kindergarten. Apparently, I used to masturbate in class by rubbing myself against the edges of chairs and tables. The teacher thought it would be best if my mom was there to make me stop. FML

Today I unexpectedly got my period at lacrosse practice. Our playing field is a half-mile run from any bathrooms, so I headed toward the woods with a tampon. Just as I was about to insert the tampon, the entire boys' cross-country team ran by . . . laughing. FML

Today I went to my new doctor, so I had to do some paperwork. As I filled out the questionnaire, she asked if I was sexually active. I said yes. She then asked, "What do you do?" I told her I normally did vaginal but would sometimes do anal. She blushed and started to laugh. She was asking where I worked. FML

Today I had a meeting with my super-hot teaching assistant. When I got to her office, she complimented me for being early, to which I thoughtfully replied, "Oh, I usually come early." She laughed. FML

It's Just Not Fair!

All around us, there are many unlucky souls who
seem to get kicked in the ass without really asking for
it. We'd be inclined to reach out to them, to tell them in
a soothing voice that things are going to be okay . . .
except that we're overcome by the urge to laugh at
their predicament. Which might not be very nice, but,
hey, it's funny!

Today my elderly neighbor gave me puppy eyes so I'd lug her seven bags full of groceries up three flights of stairs. Afterward, very grateful, she took out her purse, handed me a coin, and told me that maybe this way I could afford to "get a better haircut next time." FML

Today I found the password to my boyfriend's chat account. I was listed in the "booty call" category. FML

Today I went skinny-dipping with my best friend. We were on the beach and it was fairly crowded, but we got in the water at a really secluded area. While we were swimming, I looked up to see a homeless man wearing my clothes and walking away. FML

Today, when my husband got home from work, I was standing in the kitchen, wearing nothing but stilettos. He asked me to make him hot chocolate. FML

It's Just Not Fair!

Today I got back from a six-month deployment overseas. My girl-friend of three years couldn't pick me up from the airport because she had an intramural softball game to go to. FML

Today I was napping in my room when my dog started to bark obnoxiously. He does this all the time, so I ignored it. It went on for about a half hour. When I went downstairs, I found an open door and an empty TV stand. FML

Today, for the first time ever, I finally met someone with the same first name as me. I'm twenty years old; he is ninety-seven. FML

Today I began to undress my wife, who was watching TV, and gave her a massage to relax her while she watched her soap. Twenty minutes later, when the show came to an end, she said, "I wish you'd let me watch TV in peace!" FML

Today I gave a hand to a charming and
sweet old lady to help her cross the
road. Once we reached the other side,
she knocked into the edge of the sidewalk and I couldn't hold on to her.
She screamed, "You fucking son of a
bitch!" at me from the ground. FML

Today, as I was pressed for time, I opened some canned
food for dinner. When my children were served, they said,
"Mmm, this is best meal you've ever cooked for us!" I cook
healthy, balanced meals every day. FML

Today I decided to go to my ex-girlfriend's house to bring her
stuff back. We had broken up earlier this week after a two-year
relationship, and I'd hoped she would have realized her mistake
and asked me to stay for a bit and talk. I rang the doorbell, and
her new boyfriend opened the door. FML

Today my boss asked me, "Can I give you some constructive
criticism?" I said yes. He told me, "Your work is really shit.
You have no talent, and I can't figure out why I hired you."
FML

Today I was babysitting four rather noisy and rowdy kids. After a two-hour struggle, I finally managed to get them into bed. I asked them what they wanted before going to sleep, and the eldest replied, "Can you tell us a story where you die at the end?" FML

Today, while pumping gas, I stopped to think about what a failure my life is and how badly I've treated people in my past. Deep in thought, I accidentally pulled the gas pump out too far and covered myself with gasoline. FML

Today I tried to cuddle Simon, my five-year-old son. He wriggled away and said, "If you need a teddy bear, go buy one! Or find another Simon!" FML

Today, although my two favorite things in the world are pizza and beer, I discovered I have celiac disease and can never have either of them. FML

Today a work colleague announced that she is organizing a party. In front of everyone, she said that I'm not invited, to "avoid ruining the vibe." FML

Today I found a bone in my sandwich. It was a veggie burger. FML

Today I stepped in dog shit, barefoot, in my own bathroom. The dog had been outside for two hours previously, and I had watched him shit. Apparently, he was saving one up for when he got back in the house. FML

Today I was jerking off, and my cat jumped from out of nowhere and dug his claws into my shaft. My attempt to knock him away resulted in three nasty gashes . . . that I now have to explain to my wife. FML

It's Just Not Fair!

Today I walked into the kitchen and accidentally broke my mother's vase. I said, "Accidents happen." She replied, "Yeah, like your birth." FML

Today my boyfriend came to visit me for my birthday. Over dinner he handed me a blank card that had the words "I love you" hastily written on it. When the waiter came to take our order, my boyfriend informed him that we'd be paying separately. Happy birthday. FML

Today my family and I watched the video of my birth for the first time. In the video, when my mother sees me for the first time, she says, "God, he's ugly!" FML

Today my nineteen-year-old girlfriend dumped me because she thinks I'm immature. I'm thirty. FML

Today a really attractive woman I've
known for years told me that when
I can have sex with her standing
up, she'll have sex with me. I'm
confined to a wheelchair. FML

Today I decided to give things a go with the guy who has had a crush on me for three years, based purely on my looks. After getting to know my personality, he decided he no longer likes me at all. FML

Today I'm sick. I got a flu shot for the first time ever this year, and for the first time in my life, I have the flu. FML

Today I picked up my cat, not realizing he was sleeping, and he went wild. I ended up with several cuts, one on my wrist. Later, a kid in my high school saw my wrist and told the guidance counselor, who then told my parents. Now everyone thinks I'm either a liar, an attention whore, or emo. FML

Today my grandmother, who has Alzheimer's disease and can't usually remember my name, had a sudden moment of clarity and asked me why I'm not married yet. FML

Today my girlfriend and I broke up. She told me I just wasn't her type, but she gave me the phone number of one of her friends. Since all the friends I had met were pretty hot, I called the number later. It was a guy. FML

Today I found out that my assistant is now my manager. FML

Today I told my mom I was excited that my boobs were getting bigger. She told me that that's what happens when you get fat. FML

Today my little sister and I were reading a book together, and out of nowhere she said, "I love you." My heart melted, and I told her that I loved her, too. Then she told me that she was talking to her stuffed animal, not me. FML

Today I asked my mother if she thought my cat was getting fat. She replied, "It's not the cat you should worry about." FML

Today I drove an hour in a rainstorm to see my boyfriend. Thirty minutes and a blow job later, he told me he was going to meet some friends for dinner in half an hour, then he kicked me out of his house. It was still raining. FML

Today I realized that, due to my recent loss of appetite, instead of losing weight from my thighs as I had hoped, I've actually been losing weight from my already-small breasts. FML

Today I found out that my girlfriend's computer password is "i_love_mike." My name is not Mike. FML

Today, while surfing Facebook, I noticed that someone in my network had recently shifted his relationship status from undeclared to "single." We've been dating exclusively for nine months. FML

Today I walked past a girl in the cafeteria, and she threw up. Naturally, a crowd gathered. Her friend asked her what was wrong. She pointed at me and said, "Get him away from me!" I had never met this girl. FML

Today I was at a strip club. I put my dollar on the stage. When the stripper came over to take it, she stood me up, flipped my tits, and said I had bigger ones than she did. I'm a guy. FML

Today my sweetheart came around to drop off some underwear, which I'd left at his house. Not all of what he brought was mine. FML

Today I had sex with a girl who cried out as she came, "Forgive me, Lord! Forgive me, Lord!" FML

Today, while copying some stuff for school, I felt someone rubbing her boobs against my back. I got a boner, and when I looked to see who the hot chick was, I saw my fat friend rubbing his man-boobs against my back. FML

Today I found out that my teacher writes descriptions next to people's names on the class register to remind him who people are. By mistake, the descriptions appeared on the computer projector. Next to my name, it said "Tubby." FML

Today on my way to class I walked past a man handing out miniature Bibles. He proceeded to hand me one, commenting, "Here, you look like you need this." FML

Today I told the guy I have feelings for that I'm interested in him and asked how he feels about it. He responded, "I feel fairly neutral about that." FML

Today I caught one of my cats humping my huge dog while he was asleep. I'm sleeping with the door closed from now on. FML

Today I went to work dressed in my best outfit because my company was throwing a huge party. During the lunch break my boss said to me, "You really missed some party yesterday—it was great fun!" FML

Today I went to my boyfriend's workplace to surprise him. When I got there, I called him on his phone to tell him to turn around. I watched him look at his phone and decide not to pick up. His co-worker next to him asked who was calling. He replied, "Just this fat chick I know." FML

Today a Girl Scout asked me to
buy cookies. She looked nice, so
I bought five boxes from her. She
took the money and left with her
mom. I opened the boxes when I got
home and realized that they just had
rocks in them. I was scammed by a
Girl Scout. FML

Today my company hired a new guy to help on our project. My boss said that he would shadow me for the whole day so he could learn our system. At the end of the day, my boss fired me, handing my company car keys and laptop to my "shadow for the day" right in front of me. My mom picked me up. FML

Today I took my dog to the vet, and she was diagnosed with obesity. The vet then told me that dogs usually imitate their owners' eating and behavior habits. FML

Today my boyfriend told me he was going to take me out somewhere special, so I called in sick to work. It turned out that he had made reservations for the restaurant I worked at. FML

Today I told my mom I loved her a lot. Her reply? "Thanks." FML

Today I went with the girl I love to visit my parents out of state for the first time. My father grinned and acknowledged that she was a "keeper," at which she laughed and said we were "just friends." I was going to propose to her next week. FML

Today, for our eight-month anniversary, my boyfriend bought me a hideous necklace with ugly charms hanging off it. I wore it anyway and got a rash from it on the side of my neck. After seeing the rash, my boyfriend accused me of having a hickey from another guy. He broke up with me. FML

Today, when we were driving to dinner, my boyfriend was tapping on my thigh to the beat of the music. When I asked him what he was doing, he replied, "Just watching the ripples." FML

Today I told my mom I loved her, and she asked if I was going to kill myself. FML

F My Life

Today my boss asked me to pick up an extra shift. I said I couldn't because I had a date. He told me I didn't need to lie and to just say no next time. FML

Today, in basketball practice, my coach put us in teams to run drills. He pointed to me and said, "You, go babysit my son by the stage." FML

Today I was talking to my parents about feeling insecure with my "beach body" as spring break gets closer and closer. My dad proceeded to warn me, saying, "Don't wear a gray swimsuit. People will try to roll you back into the ocean." FML

Today I accompanied some friends to sign up at a gym. When we got there, the guy handed me a form, too. I said, "Oh, I'm not signing up." He replied, "Out of all of you, you need it the most." He then said he was also a nutritionist and offered a consultation. FML

Today I told my dad I was leaving to get some beauty sleep. He looked at me, laughing, and said, "See you in a decade." FML

Today my mother decided she wanted the family to go on a special outing for the holidays. She asked me to drive everyone when she got home from work. Later I noticed the house was empty. The whole family, including the dog, had left without telling me. They took my car. FML

Today I woke up happy because I'd met the man of my dreams at a bar. We shared an amazing night together. I walked around my apartment, wondering where he'd gone. It turned out that not only was he gone, but so was my car. FML

Today my best friend slapped me and called me some colorful names before telling me that she never wanted to speak to me again because I supposedly slept with her boyfriend. Not only am I a virgin, but I'm also a lesbian. FML

Today, while at work at my grocery store, I sold a *ton* of eggs to a bunch of kids. We joked around that they were "going to bake a giant cake." When I got home I found that someone had egged my house. FML

Today, while visiting my grandmother at her nursing home, I was looking at pictures she had of all the grandkids. All of them were normal graduation pictures and so forth, but mine was a cutout in which she made me skinnier. FML

Today the girl I love told me she was sick of guys. I replied that I happened to be a guy. She laughed and said, "No, I mean the boyfriend type!" FML

Today I did my work, the work of my co-worker who had called in sick, and the work of my boss, who has no idea what the hell is going on—all at the same time. I didn't get a promotion because I don't work hard enough. FML

Today, at a strategy session, my manager displayed a flowchart of his employees. I wasn't included. Apparently I had been fired. They forgot to tell me. FML

Today I spent $20 on a spray tan, $30 to have my makeup done, and $50 on a pretty new dress, all for a special date with my boyfriend. It turns out that I spent $100 just to get dumped. FML

Today my grandmother called. She greeted me by my mother's name. When I told her it was not my mother, she apologized and corrected herself, but this time she addressed me as my sister. When I told her it was not my sister either, she said, "Sorry, wrong number," and hung up. FML

Today my boyfriend gave me a gift card for $32 to a local salon. I thought the amount was kind of random, but when I went in I saw that the bikini wax was $32. FML

Today my boyfriend and I decided to
have sex at his house. When we got
there, he checked his mailbox first
and noticed that his Wii game had
arrived. He sent me home so he could
play. FML

missbean

Today I found a note in my locker from a really hot guy, asking me to the prom. I went up to him and said how excited I was to go. He said, "Oh, *you* got the note?" He took it back and slipped it into the locker next to mine. FML

Today I told my parents I really missed them and wanted to come home for the weekend because I hadn't seen them in months. They told me that that was a bad idea and they couldn't fit me into their schedule. I asked what their plans were. They said they didn't have any yet. FML

Today my boyfriend broke up with me. He said I was way too good at sex, so I must have lied about not having much experience, and he "couldn't be with someone who is hiding something." WTF? FML

Today my boyfriend and I were in Victoria's Secret. I saw a picture of a model and said, "I wish I looked like that." He sighed and replied, "Me too." FML

It's Just Not Fair!

Today in school my shoulder was killing me from a softball injury.
I went to the nurse's office and asked, "Can I have some ice?"
The nurse responded, "Oh no, what happened to your face?" FML

Today I went for a run and took my shirt off partway through. The next person I saw was a nine-year-old girl playing outside her house. She looked at me and said, "Ewwwwww! Gross!" FML

Today my girlfriend and I were fooling around, and I was just about to reach orgasm when she looked at the clock and said, "I have to go. *Lost* is on in twenty minutes." FML

Today I went to the hair salon to cut six inches off my hair. When I got there, I decided to get my upper lip waxed for the first time. When my boyfriend came to pick me up for our date, I asked whether he noticed anything different about me. The first thing he said was "I see you got rid of your mustache." FML

Today I came back from college and visited my parents' house. There was a new portrait of my parents and two sisters hanging over the mantel. My mom had always wanted a family portrait, but she had always postponed having it done. The painting was dated the day after I had left for college. FML

Today I walked downstairs in a new outfit, after dieting for three months and losing just over twenty pounds. My mom took one look at me and said, "You'd better keep going." FML

Today my guy friend and I were in his dorm room watching a movie, when he started kissing me. Things heated up, so we moved over to his bed. He was on me, when a hand shot down from the top bunk. His roommate had been up there the whole time and wanted a high five. So they high-fived. FML

Today I went to the gym and worked out with a trainer. While I was doing arm exercises, he commented on how impressed he was with the size of my triceps. That really boosted my self-confidence, until he leaned in to feel them and said, "Oh, it's just fat." FML

Today this guy I have been in love with for two years asked me into an empty classroom. He handed me a bouquet of flowers and a T-shirt on which he had silk-screened "Prom?" I said that it was the most adorable thing I had ever seen. He asked if I thought that my best friend would like it. FML

Today I got my car fixed from an accident, and I drove to a party in a bad thunderstorm. When the power went out, everyone decided to watch the storm from the front windows. Someone mentioned that it would be funny if the tree fell on my car with everyone watching. Twenty seconds later, it did. FML

Today I passed by a small shop and decided to go in to look at the jeans. Before I could even step inside, the shop owner told me expressionlessly, "All the sizes here are too small for you." FML

Today, at a hard-rock concert, a bunch of guys accidentally knocked down a porta-potty while moshing. I was inside that porta-potty. FML

Today I had sex with my girlfriend. Being the stud that I am, after a short time I turned to her and said, "You think you're ready for a round two?" She replied, "No, but I do think I'm ready for the rest of round one." FML

Today I was questioned about a request for a restraining order filed against me by an old woman. According to the report, she's seen me "walking near her house and waving at her" for the last two months. I've been her next-door neighbor for a year and a half. FML

Today, after soccer practice, I was walking to the car with my dad. My teammates waved and said, "Bye, *Pot-head!*" They call me that because they think my head is shaped like a pot. Of course, my dad didn't believe me. I'm grounded now because I have an abnormally shaped head. I've never smoked pot. FML

Today, three days before my wedding day, I found out that my fiancé is sleeping with one of my bridesmaids. I just canceled a $200,000 wedding. I now have to help my family (who flew in from Poland, California, and Massachusetts) book flights back home. FML

Today, while I was driving my kids to school, my son said, "Why don't you find another place to live, so we can just live with Daddy?" Then my daughter added, "Yeah, 'cause we *love* Daddy." FML

Today I proposed to my girlfriend, whom I was madly in love with, by having a plane fly over her house spelling out "Marry me, Abby?" After seeing this, she locked herself in her room and cried for four hours, exclaiming that this wasn't how she wanted to be proposed to. I had invited my entire family to see it. FML

Today I got braces. When we got in the car, my dad looked over and said, "Well, at least we don't have to worry about boys for the next two years." FML

Today I was walking through the mall with my boyfriend of a year and a half. There was a sign outside a jewelry store that said "Engagement Rings—No interest for 12 months." I said, "Look, baby! No interest." He replied, "That's right . . . *no interest*." FML

Today I went swimming. As I was
getting out of the very crowded
pool, a little girl ran up to me,
pointed, and yelled, "Mommy, I want
big boobies like that when I grow
up." I'm sixteen. I'm a boy. FML

missbean

Today I finally told my best friend, whom I've secretly been in love with for two years, that I was in love with her, but at the last second I chickened out and said I was joking. She replied, "Don't scare me like that. For a second, I thought I was going to have to find a new best friend." FML

Today I was in the bank with my seven-year-old daughter, when I saw an old high school friend of mine with his wife. I said hello, and he commented on how beautiful my little girl was. I thanked him, and as I turned away I heard his wife say, "I guess the father must be the good-looking one." FML

Today I went to get a physical. The nurse was morbidly obese and unattractive. She told me she would go through the tests listed on the sheet. She did everything, including feeling my genitalia. When it was done, I read over the sheet. Genitalia wasn't one of the tests listed. FML

Today I was lying on the couch with my girlfriend. I looked at her and said, "You're so beautiful. How did I ever get you?" She replied, "I was drunk." FML

Today I was serving a table full of drunk people. They used the candles on the table to set the table on fire. Noticing this, I ran to it and poured a pitcher of water on it. Then other tables complained, saying I had caused a disturbance. I got fired for putting out a fire. FML

Today I was at a party, and we were all playing Seven Minutes in Heaven. It was my crush's turn to spin the bottle, so my heart started pounding. The bottle pointed toward me! Then my crush said, "With her, it'd be 'Seven Minutes in Hell.' Just skip me." FML

Today I went to get my eyebrows waxed at a Korean salon. I had never been there before, and it was hard to understand their accents. The women asked me whether I wanted "them all off." Not fully understanding what she had said, I agreed. When she showed me the mirror, she had taken off my whole eyebrow. FML

Today my wife and I were driving to a gas station. She let me out before she pulled up to the pump because I had to buy some things from the store. I returned to see my wife proudly filling the tank, something she never does. Smiling, she told me that diesel was cheaper than regular gas. We don't own a diesel car. FML

Today, for our two-year anniversary,
I got my girlfriend a very expensive
diamond necklace. She got me male
enhancement pills. FML

Today I drove my two kids to their friends' houses. In my convertible, looking what I thought was my best, I slowed down outside a bar with a group of cute twenty-year-old girls out front. My daughter noticed the speed reduction and said, "Keep driving, Dad. You're fat, and Mom left you for a reason." FML

Today my best friend, whom I have been secretly in love with forever, was ranting about her ex-girlfriend. Then she said, "If only you were gay, we'd be perfect for each other." So I took the chance to tell her that I was. She responded, "Well, I'm still not attracted to you." FML

Today I went to visit my grandmother, accidentally leaving my cell phone at home for the weekend. When I got back, I had two texts from my crush. One said, "I want to take the most beautiful girl to prom, go with me?" The other said, "Fine, fatty, I'll ask someone else." FML

Today I was picking up my daughter from my ex-husband's house, and his new girlfriend was there. I called to my daughter that it was time to leave, and she clung to his girlfriend, saying, "Mommy, I don't want to leave." She wasn't talking to me. FML

Today all of my friends and teachers asked me what was wrong because I looked sad and tired. One kid even said that I looked like "an abused housewife the day after." I was fine. It was the first time I had gone to school without wearing any makeup. FML

Today I was sitting in a restaurant with my best friend. We had competed in a pageant together earlier this month. A lady came up to my friend, who had been named first alternate, and said,"You were robbed of that title. You deserved to win. I hated the winner." I was the winner. FML

Today I sent an email to my best friend, telling him that I'm gay. When I was typing the email address in the "To:" field, I didn't notice, but it autocorrected to my mother's address. She just responded, "You filthy faggot." FML

Today I was walking from my office to the place I had parked my car, a distance of approximately three blocks. As I was about to round the last corner, I was forced to dive out of the way of a speeding car. I looked up and noticed that it was my car. FML

Today, when a bartender carded my friends, I excitedly asked whether he was going to card me. The guy gave me a blank stare before finally replying, "Look, lady, I don't have time to stroke some middle-aged woman's ego." I had asked because it was my birthday. I just turned twenty-one. FML

Today I was at a dance. I was grinding with this guy, when I felt something move in his pants. I stood up and stepped away. He replied, "Don't flatter yourself. It was my phone." FML

Today I arrived at work, only to be arrested and accused of stealing over $8,000 from my employer. Five hours later, at the police station, the discovery was made that the actual thief had an employee ID that was one digit different from mine. He works at another location more than 1,200 miles away. FML

Today I emailed the guy I like to ask him on a coffee date. He declined by telling me he never drinks coffee. We had met at Starbucks. FML

Today my boss had to leave the house for a little while. She asked me to take any messages she got. I answered the phone, and the lady calling said she was returning my boss's call about the opening for a nanny position. I am the current nanny. I found out from the new nanny that I was being fired. FML

Today my boss told me that I had been hired because of how much I reminded him of his daughter. Taking this as a compliment, I mentioned it to a co-worker whom I was trying to impress. I later found out that my boss's daughter is both clinically obese and mentally challenged. FML

Today I was pulled over because I looked like a possible suspect in a robbery. While he was searching me, the police radio went off and the person on the other end said, "Possible suspect, five foot five, thin." The officer stopped abruptly, murmuring, "Too short and fat," and walked back to his car. FML

Today my boyfriend handcuffed me
to the bed, naked. Someone pulled
the fire alarm, and my boyfriend
couldn't find the key to the
cuffs. So he left me there, and
the resident advisor found me. A
fireman had to cut the chain. FML

Today my brother's new girlfriend, who is blind, asked to feel my face so she could tell what I look like. She said I was "unique." A blind chick told me I was ugly. FML

Today I was walking to school and decided to be a good citizen by picking up a beer can on the sidewalk. I then walked onto my school's campus, where I got suspended by the dean for "trying to rebel," got grounded by my parents for getting suspended, and got a "minor in possession" ticket from school security. FML

Today I was shopping with my friends, and a man asked me whether I would be in one of his commercials. I said yes without thinking twice. Then I found out that he wanted me to be the "before" picture for an acne control cream. FML

Today I walked up behind a girl I had hooked up with last weekend while she was working at a computer in the library. I noticed that she was looking at my Facebook page, and I got excited. Then I heard her say to her friend, "This guy has the smallest penis I have ever seen." FML

Today I heard back from my store manager interview at Target. I was offered an overnight stock clerk position. When I called the human resources department to find out if my application was in the wrong file, I was told that I lack the leadership qualities necessary for Target. I graduated with honors from a military school. FML

Today, at the dinner table, my parents were talking to my younger sister about her new boyfriend and how they should be taking it slow. My sister pointed out that that's not what I do. My dad said, "Believe me, I know—your sister's easier to get into than community college." FML

Today my boss wanted to promote me to a managerial position. I declined the position, saying I didn't think I was ready and experienced enough for that role. I was then fired instead for not accepting the promotion. I was fired for being honest. FML

Today I finally got the courage to tell my best friend that I've had a crush on him since our junior year. Since I couldn't see him, I sent him a text. His response: "Yeah, I know. I've tried kind of ignoring it." FML

Today my first girlfriend of over
three years left me for another guy.
She said she's looking for someone
who can financially provide for her in
the future. He owns a T-Mobile kiosk.
I'm going to medical school. FML

Today I told my boyfriend, "We need to talk." He said, "I
know." So we met after school, and he said he was okay with
me breaking up with him, that he wasn't that into me, either.
He said all that before I could tell him that my parents wanted
to meet him. FML

Today, after work, I went to the parking lot to my car to go
home. I found my car doors heavily scratched and all my tires
slashed, and a note on my windshield. The note read: "Fuck
you, Jackson. Don't fuck with me." I'm Tyler. Jackson is my
co-worker. FML

You Shouldn't Have Even Bothered . . .

You've got to play to win, as they say. But for some people, success is *not* always waiting just around the corner. This can be a good thing for the rest of us, because there's something amusing about watching your peers fail miserably. "A problem shared is a problem halved." That may very well be, but we'll stick to the other half of the equation, the one where we pour scorn onto those unlucky objects of ridicule.

Today I wanted to see whether the frying pan was hot. I no longer have fingerprints. FML

Today I was hitting on a girl who was getting ready to walk into the same class as I was. We were waiting outside the room, and I told her that I had heard that the professor for the course was a total bitch. We walked into the room. I sat down at a desk. She stood behind the podium. FML

Today, while shaving, I cut myself. With the blade protector. FML

Today I was on a date with my new boyfriend. I acted very flirty and laughed very loudly to show him how funny he was. I laughed so loudly that I farted. FML

Today, after a tremendously hot night with a guy I had met the night before, I asked him his phone number. He replied, "What for?" FML

Today, in a hallway at college, to make my friends laugh, I was joking about how I'd had passionate sex with our professor. Just then, the professor passed right behind me, reminding me of the date of my next oral exam. She will be grading me. FML

Today I told myself: "Go on, you big geek, go outside, get some sun, get your ass away from your computer, go for a walk." I finally mustered the courage to leave my house. Without my keys. I've been in an Internet café for four hours. FML

Today my mistress called my wife. FML

Today, feeling romantic and overwhelmed with love, I told my fiancée, "I don't know what I'd do without you." She replied, "Well, you'd jerk off." FML

Today, and for the last eight months, my upstairs neighbors have been making a tremendous racket. I finally decided to go up and complain: "The amount of noise you make is unbelievable! It sounds like you're riding tractors up here!" The woman replied, "My husband is a paraplegic." FML

Today we were out walking around and smoking a bit of weed. We saw a place to sit down in a little parking lot nearby. The cops came over and busted us. It turned out that we were in the main lot for the police station. FML

Today my son looked out the window and said, "What's that piece of shit doing in our driveway?" It was the new car we were planning to surprise him with on his birthday. FML

Today my girlfriend and I went to a club. When the song "Single Ladies" by Beyoncé played, the DJ came on the mic and said, "Single ladies, raise your hands!" My girlfriend raised her hand. FML

Today my husband came home from work angry. He started yelling about how much he hates the neighbor's kids and that he never wants to have children. Tonight I was going to tell him that I'm pregnant. FML

Today I had to go to my son's school for career day. I explained what a banker does, and then I asked if any-one had a question. One boy raised his hand and asked, "When are all the cool parents gonna come?" FML

Today, at the Golden Gate Bridge, I spotted a large group of Asian people trying to take a group photograph. Trying to be helpful, I slowly said, "You . . . want me . . . take picture?" while using hand motions. The man looked at me and said, "No thanks, asshole. I got it," in perfect English. FML

Today I lied and said I was late for work because I had a flat tire. Two hours later, some of my friends came in and said in front of my manager, "We should do brunch every Saturday, like this morning. It was awesome!" FML

Today I was driving after dark and saw a small animal run across the road. I slammed on my brakes and got rear-ended. The animal turned out to be a plastic grocery bag. FML

Today I went shopping with a girl I like while my girlfriend was busy. We ended up going grocery shopping to make dinner together, and I ran into my girlfriend's parents. FML

Today, after I'd been looking for my cell phone for two days, I realized that the vegetable compartment in the fridge was vibrating. FML

Today, wanting a change from the usual pizza-and-Coke menu, I decide to cook. After spending an hour and a half making a beef chili with ancho, mole, and cumin, I was sprinkling a bit of salt on top of it, and the top came off the saltshaker. FML

Today, when I was out with my boyfriend, I walked ahead of him catwalk style. I turned around and asked, "Do you think I could model?" He blurted out, "Yes . . . for a plus-size clothing line." FML

Today I decided to quit smoking and put on a nicotine patch. I decided to have one last cigarette, and ended up at the doctor's office, sick with nicotine poisoning. FML

Today I won $5,000 on a lottery ticket and tried giving the man next to me a high five. He had no hands. FML

Today, I was making a smoothie. I
didn't plug in the blender until
after all the ingredients were
inside. It was still on when I
plugged it in...with no lid. FML

Today, while walking in the woods, I hit my foot against a half-buried metal object. I dug into the ground and found a beautiful box, heavy enough not to be empty. I imagined myself rich with gold coins. It was the corpse of a dead cat. FML

Today I was rejected from the University of Washington. My dad has been a professor there for thirty years, and he is on the board of admissions. FML

Today I made fun of my friend when she tripped over a curb. I said loudly, "Haha, you can't even walk." Then I noticed the man in the wheelchair a few feet ahead of us. FML

Today I was masturbating in the bottom bunk of my bunk beds. When I finished and tried to get up to clean myself, I hit my head on the metal panel of the upper bunk and passed out. My parents came home and found me passed out, naked and holding a porn magazine. FML

Today I went to a party with the boy I am interested in. It was the first time I had met his friends. It turned out that he and all his friends are hard-core Christians who don't drink and are celibate. FML

Today I promised my best friend that I wouldn't let her hook up with any guys, since she got an STD a few weeks ago. After we tossed a few back, she led about thirty people in a chant of "cockblock" after I wouldn't let her go home with some random dude. FML

Today my husband of nine years announced he was gay. He insinuated that he was able to achieve erections only because I looked like a man. FML

Today I saw a homeless man asking for money. Not wanting to give him any because he'd just spend it on booze, I decided to buy him a full Big Mac meal from McDonald's. When I went to hand it to him, he waved his hand, refusing it and saying, "Thanks, but I'm a vegetarian." FML

Today I got caught stealing lollipops. I am twenty-five. FML

Today I was finally able to get to know a girl I'd been eyeing for months. We had a nice conversation. We discovered that we live in the same area, so we talked about that. I told her that the little restaurant under my apartment was really disgusting. Her parents own it. FML

Today, I was the photographer at my friend's wedding. I took stupid pictures all day long. The moment the bride entered the church, the battery in my camera died. FML

Today I went to surprise my boyfriend in the shower. I opened the door, and there was a giant turd in the toilet. I pretended I was looking for my hairbrush. FML

Today my overprotective mom decided to do a blacklight test on my room to make sure I wasn't doing the naughty. The bed was clean. My face wasn't. FML

Today I was bored while I was pooping, so I decided to paint my nails. I had to wait thirty minutes to wipe. FML

Today I was at work at the Disney Store. A little boy was crying, so I went over to comfort him. After talking to him for a little while, I found out that he couldn't find his mother. When he calmed down, I went to help him stand up. He choked back his tears and then puked all over me from the waist down. FML

Today I was having sex with my girlfriend, and as I pulled out to finish I slipped and ended up punching her in the stomach. I came while she was writhing in pain. FML

Today I decided to make a Pop-Tart. I thought it was bad enough when it fell through the grate in the toaster oven. Then it burst into flames. I spent five minutes fanning the smoke away from the smoke detector, but the alarm continued to go off. Now everyone who lives in my building is outside in a snowstorm. FML

Today I was at a bar in Canada and was really hitting it off with a girl. She asked how big my junk was and I told her, in inches. They use centimeters. FML

Today a toddler's ball rolled over to me in the park. I playfully pitched it to him, as his parents watched from afar. The ball hit him in the face. FML

Today I thought I was giving a woman the orgasm of a lifetime until I realized that she was telling me to stop pulling her hair. FML

Today I buried my girlfriend's recently deceased cat. Later she asked to see the grave and then came back inside, crying. I hadn't buried it completely. Its two back legs were poking out of the dirt. FML

Today I broke up with my boyfriend. I called him two minutes after I left, and he had already fallen asleep. FML

Today I was looking at porn on my laptop when my mom came into my room to talk to me. After she had finished what she was saying, she paused and said, "You know, I can see the reflection of your computer screen in your glasses." FML

Today my girlfriend snuck up behind me to cover my eyes and play "Guess who." The second her hands touched my face, I instinctively grabbed her, twisted her wrists, and kneed her to the floor. FML

Today I slept with this new guy for the first time. After sex, he said the doggie style was fun; it reminded him of what it was like to rape a girl. FML

Today my girlfriend asked if her friend Alex, from high school, could join us for an amazing threesome. As a horny dude, how could I say no? It turned out that Alex is also a guy's name. FML

Today I was watching a porn video on my laptop when my mom walked into my room, so I slammed the laptop shut. The speakers continued to function after the laptop was closed. FML

Today I decided to get in shape. I went to the store to buy some free weights. I couldn't take them home. The box was too heavy. FML

Today I tried helping an old lady with her groceries. When I asked if she needed help, she smiled. When I took one of her bags, she yelled. She was deaf. FML

Today I finally mustered the balls to skip out of class early, only to find that the back door was locked. As I stood there like an idiot trying to get it open, all two hundred people in my class turned to laugh. My professor stared at me. I went back to my seat, sat down, and took out my notebook. FML

Today, after a late night at the bars, I got into my building's elevator with a Chinese man who was carrying a plastic bag. Excited, I asked, "Oooh, are you still delivering?" He replied, "I live here." FML

Today I was taking the elevator down, and it was full of people. It stopped on the second floor, and before the doors opened, I said, "What asshole can't take the steps from the second floor?" A kid in a wheelchair got on. FML

Today my boyfriend and I decided to
try anal sex. When he was done, I
turned around to see that he was
holding a strap-on. With a smile on
his face, he said, "Now, do me." FML

Today a woman walked out of the Humane Society with a cat carrier. I asked her, "Oh, did you adopt him?" She walked past me and started crying. She had just brought her cat in to be euthanized. FML

Today I had a sexy dream, woke up, and started to masturbate quite vigorously. When I finished, I hopped off the top bunk, naked, to see my brother and his girlfriend lying in the bottom bunk, awake. FML

Today I went on a first date with an Egyptian-Cuban girl. I asked her what language she was brought up speaking. She said that her mom spoke to her in Spanish, but that she only ever replied in English. I said, "Oh, kinda like Chewbacca and Han Solo?" FML

Today I was driving and stopped behind another car. The driver didn't move for at least a minute. I got out of my car, yelling at the person. It was an old woman. She wasn't breathing. FML

Today I found out that when I masturbate at night while watching Internet porn, I cast a huge shadow on the curtain and the entire street is able to see it. FML

Today I went to a movie with my boyfriend. In the lobby, I asked why the glasses were not working. My boyfriend replied, "3-D glasses just work for the movie; everything else in the world is pretty much already 3-D." FML

Today I spent almost my entire English class turned on, thinking that the hot girl next to me was playing footsie with me. That is, until she stood up and I realized I had been rubbing my foot on her backpack. FML

Today I noticed that a prospective employer I had been networking with had changed her last name on her email signature. I wished the acquaintance congratulations on her marriage. Her divorce was finalized this week. FML

Today my entire family sat down in the living room to watch the video I had recorded of my sister's college graduation. It turned out that I had never hit Record. FML

Today I tried hallucinogenic mushrooms for the first time, with my friend. Little did I know, the effect lasts for around six hours, and I had class at three, when I had to give a presentation in front of thirty people. FML

Today I asked my boss for a raise. He responded by saying, "Who the hell are you?" FML

Today I cut myself on a Band-Aid box, while trying to get a Band-Aid out for another cut. FML

Today I changed the C on my report card into a B so I wouldn't get in trouble with my parents. I spent the entire day perfecting the B's positioning, cutting exactly around the edges of the size ten font, and I sliced my finger in the process. I was grounded for getting a B. FML

Today, while alone in the communal showers in the high school football locker room, I jokingly started to swing my penis around. Two minutes later the rest of the team hopped into the shower. Thirty dudes, one self-induced boner. FML.

Today I told the man I'm sleeping with that I thought my sister was prettier than me. He replied, "Not significantly." FML

Today I woke up next to my girlfriend. When she asked me to pick up her thong from behind my bed, I realized that there were two thongs there. I didn't pick up hers. FML

Today my husband found the box my morning-after pill came in. He had a vasectomy ten years ago. FML

Today I was doing a PowerPoint presentation for the management committee. Outlook Express was still open, and right in the middle of the presentation a window popped up notifying me of a new message. The subject line read: "RE: your job application for the post of Marketing Manager." FML

Today my husband invited his new boss and the boss's wife to dinner. During the meal, I tasted the wine and apologized for its bad quality. Somewhat annoyed, I announced, "Don't drink that. I'll go and look for another bottle." Our guests had brought the wine. FML

Today, in front of a hospital, I noticed that an old lady was having trouble lighting her cigarette because she had Parkinson's disease. I helped her to light up, and she started chatting with me. She told me she had lung cancer. FML

Today I was on a transatlantic flight with earplugs in my ears. The steward walked past with a plastic bag. I threw my litter into it and didn't immediately understand why he said, "Very funny, sir." It wasn't trash—he was collecting for UNICEF. FML

Today I went to fill up my car. Five hundred feet before the gas station, I saw a motorcycle gang in my rearview mirror. I slowed down and pulled over to let them pass. They were going to fill up, too. Thirty-five motorcycles and two gas pumps. FML

Today I was walking my son to school. After scolding him for not looking where he was going, I grabbed his hand and pulled him closer to me . . . and I walked him right into a light pole. FML

Today I met a guy who said he thinks he's in love with my sister. As a joke, I told him that my sister cheats on everyone. I got home to find my sister crying, because some-one had told her boyfriend that she's cheating on him. FML

Today I went to my friend's house
to smoke weed while his parents
were out. Forty-five minutes into
smoking, his parents called to say
they'd be home in five minutes. We
decided to spray the house with
Febreze to mask the smell. We were
high and in a rush. It was bug
spray. FML

Today, on a crowded train, a cute guy
called me over and told me to stand
next to him because there were fewer
people there. We started talking, but
he left before I could get his number.
I was about to call my friends to tell
them about him, when I realized that
he had stolen my phone. FML

Today I was helping to supervise a five-year-old's birthday
party in an inflatable obstacle course. I was playing hide-and-
seek with the kids. I saw the birthday boy and crept around
the corner, yelling, "Found you!" I scared him so much that he
peed his pants in front of everyone. FML

Today I closed out of a video chat with my boyfriend to go take
a shit. I took my computer with me to check my email. It took
five minutes for me to realize I was still on video chat. FML

Today at work I spent three minutes struggling to uncork a
wine bottle for one of my tables, only to have the diners point
out to me that the bottle was a twist-off. FML

Today I saw my male boss holding a purse. Just to be a smart-ass, I made fun of him as if the purse was his. It was. FML

Today I was playing musical chairs at a family reunion. It's a well-known fact that I'm competitive and tend to hip-check people to get that last chair. It came down to me and Nana. I won. Nana has a broken hip. FML

Today I was a host during a kids' event. I started to do some funny moves to entertain the kids. I was wearing a low-cut top. Then I noticed that all the children were pointing at me happily and the adults looked shocked. Both my boobs had popped out. FML

Today I was pulled over by a bike cop for speeding in a twenty-five-mile-per-hour zone. As the cop walked toward my car, I flicked my cigarette butt out of my window. He wrote me two tickets instead of one. FML

Today I walked by my roommate and his girlfriend while they were hugging. I asked, "What's up, lovebirds?" They were in the middle of breaking up. FML

Today I drank a ton of beers for my twenty-fifth birthday. My friends love to watch me open beer bottles with my teeth. I chipped both of my front uppers doing this. Twenty-five is the age at which I'm no longer covered by my parents' dental insurance. FML

Today I lost $200 playing poker while wearing my new shades. It turned out that you can see the cards in the reflection on the lenses. FML

Today I was at church and saw a blind teenager who obviously felt lost. Feeling like I should help, I went over and asked if he needed anything. He said, "I can't find my caretaker." I asked, "What does she look like?" FML

Today I went in for my second day at my new internship. My bosses greeted me and told me we were going to have a meeting. The meeting was to listen to the voice mails I had left them on Saturday when I was drunk. FML

Today, in front of the entire family, I yelled at my mom and told her she wasn't a good parent. She replied, "Well, at least I had friends when I was your age." FML

Today I was hooking up with a girl in my apartment, and I told her I didn't have a condom. She responded by laughing in my face. When she noticed my look of confusion, she said, "Oh, you actually thought I'd have sex with you?" FML

Today I was at the airport, about to listen to Disney's *Camp Rock* soundtrack on my iPhone. I pressed Play, only to realize a minute later that my headphones weren't plugged in all the way. Everyone sitting near me heard Joe Jonas's voice. I am forty years old. FML

Today I saw my friend across campus. I decided that I wanted to play a trick on her and scare her from behind. It turned out that I scared a complete stranger who has really bad panic-induced asthma. FML.

Today I kneeled down to tie my shoe and sneezed, nailing my face on my knee and breaking my nose. FML

Today I studied for thirteen and a half hours, completely outlining a book for history class. Thirty minutes before the test, I realized it was the wrong book. FML

Today my five-year-old nephew showed me green Martians he had made with his new Play-Doh set. I smiled and said, "Wow! Now, how about some blue Martians?" He looked at me and replied, "How about some blue shut the fuck up?" FML

Today I was secretly listening to a voice mail from my mom in math class, when I accidentally hit the speakerphone button. My whole math class now knows that I have a gynecologist appointment at 9:45 on March 11. FML

Today I saw an elderly man fall in a crosswalk, so I jumped off my bike to help. As I helped him across the street, the light turned green. At that point I noticed that my phone had fallen out of my pocket and had been run over by several cars. I then watched from across a six-lane street as someone stole my bike. FML

Today I got into a fight with one of my closest friends. She ended the conversation by saying, "My grandma just had a stroke. Bye." I didn't believe her, so I replied, "That's great! Bye." Her grandma is in critical condition. FML

Today in class my friend played a joke on me by pulling my seat out from under me when I was about to sit down. I fell, and everybody laughed at me. During the next class I did the same thing to him, and he broke his arm. He is the star of the basketball team. Nobody laughed. FML

Today I drunk-dialed my mom and told her I was so high and drunk that I thought the KGB was coming after me. When I woke up this morning, my mom told me that she is no longer paying for college. FML

Today I called the florist and ordered a flower arrangement for my grandma, who, I had been told, was sick. I didn't know what to get her, so I told them to just send her something nice. I got a call from my mom, who told me I was an inconsiderate bastard. The florist had sent my grandma forget-me-nots. She has Alzheimer's disease. FML

Today I went to the store to buy some condoms for my girlfriend and me. I was in a rush, and when I looked at the cashier, I realized it was my girlfriend's father. Nervous and hoping to reassure him, I stuttered, "Don't worry, I'm not using these with Kim." That didn't help. FML

Today I sent notes to three hundred friends saying that I'm having a birthday party in a couple weeks. I asked them to RSVP if they were interested in coming. Two people answered. They couldn't make it. FML

Today I decided to try a new cardio workout video. As I was obnoxiously bouncing around my room, I heard something behind me. Three adolescent boys were outside my window, watching. FML

Today I visited my brother in jail for the first time. I didn't know what to say, so I blurted out "Having fun?" FML

Today I had the cops called on me because I accidentally texted "I'm going to kill you and use your head as a hood ornament" to my ex-fiancé instead of to my best friend, who had gotten a better grade on an exam than I did. I now have a court date. FML

Today I was in an elevator with my girlfriend, when it got stuck midfloor. Being supportive, I went to hug her and tell her we'd be okay. Today I also learned that my girlfriend is claustrophobic and her predominant reaction is to vomit. All over me. We were stuck for two hours. FML

Today my girlfriend tried to clean
out the fireplace with a vacuum
cleaner, and she sucked up a bunch
of embers, which set the vacuum
cleaner on fire. After crying for
a bit, she went back to finish
cleaning up, only to find that some
embers she had dumped in a bucket
had melted through and set part of
the carpet on fire. FML

Today after class I was chatting with my teacher, a really cool and stylish old black guy. I told him that he reminds me of one of those soul dudes from the '70s movies, right down to the "pimp-walk." He told me he walks that way because he was beaten for drinking out of the wrong fountain as a kid. FML

Today I was over at my boyfriend's house, and I heard a strange sound. I laughed and said, "It sounds like a dog throwing up!" He listened for a second and said, "That's my mom crying downstairs." FML

Today I asked a very cute fireman for his number "just in case I need you to come to my rescue." He told me, "Yeah, sure!" and scribbled it down. After he walked away, I read his note. It said: "911." FML

Today I was walking to a meeting and saw two girls trying to jump-start a car in the rain. Thinking I'd be a gentleman and help them, I offered to assist. The girl whose car had broken down looked at me, then looked at her friend with concern and said, "I think we'd better call the police." FML

Today I was at work, about to go to lunch. There were some Girl Scouts out front selling cookies. I told my manager that I would be using a different exit. When he asked why, I told him that Girl Scouts really annoy the crap out of me. The Girl Scouts out front were his daughters. FML

Today I was at the school's rec center, working out for the first time in a while. As I exercised, a very mysteriously attractive girl kept shooting me glances. I asked for her number, and she responded that she would give it to me "if you can lift the same weight as me." I couldn't. FML

Today the history class for which I am the teaching assistant was taking a test. About halfway through, I noticed one kid had a small piece of paper in his hand. I ran up the row, grabbed his test, and ripped it into four pieces. Then I looked at the note. It read: "I believe in you. —Mom." FML

Today a stoplight turned yellow as I was approaching it. I was about to go through, but I saw a cop, panicked, and slammed on the brakes. I ended up in the middle of the intersection and had to reverse. Soon the light turned green, and I stepped on the gas. My car was still in reverse. FML

Today I saw my ex-girlfriend across the street. I was walking with a girl whom I'd been hooking up with, and I wanted to make my ex-girlfriend jealous so I kissed the other girl and she immediately smacked me. I got a "ha-ha!" text from my ex. FML

Today I babysat a five-year-old girl. She ran up to me, threw her arms around my waist, and said, "*Yummy!* I'm going to eat you!" with her face in my crotch. I said sarcastically under my breath, "Finally, some action!" I turned around to find her dad staring at me. FML

Today, during my choral concert, I was helping to turn the pages for the pianist who was accompanying the singers. In the middle of the song, one of the pages slipped and fell into his crotch. In a panic, I frantically reached to grab the music. I grabbed something. It wasn't the music. FML

Today, when I was out walking, a man pointed a camera at me. I decided to be bitchy about it, so I said, "Did I say you could take a picture?" He replied, "No, but can you get the fuck out of the way so I can take one of my wife and kids?" I turned around. They were right behind me. FML

Today my parents left for work before I had to leave for school, and I decided to skip. I stayed by the phone, expecting the school to call so I could pose as my parent and excuse my absence. The phone rang and I picked up. It was my mom calling to leave my dad a message on the machine. FML

Today I forgot to do my French homework, but since it was an online worksheet I told my teacher that my Internet service wasn't working. I told her via email. FML

Today I was babysitting a one-year-old. She had just learned how to say yes, so if you asked her *anything,* she'd say yes. I asked her if she liked vegetables, and she said, "Yes!" Then I asked her if I was pretty. . . . She looked at me and said *"No!"* FML

Today I took my girlfriend to a very nice restaurant. I thought it would be a good place to pop the question. I gave the ring to the waiter and asked him to put it on her dessert plate. When she saw it, she picked it up, put it down, and said, "No." Then she ate the dessert. FML

Today I met a really attractive guy, who introduced himself as Wyan. He was really cool and sweet, and we got along pretty well. Later someone told me that his name is Ryan and that he has a speech impediment. Throughout the conversation I had been referring to him as Wyan. FML

Today a guy I've been on five dates with called me for the first time in two weeks. The first thing I said was, "Don't expect me to go out with you again after going AWOL on me." Then he told me his mom had died. FML

Today I went to the movies with some girlfriends. The guy behind us was making pervy heavy-breathing noises, so we threw some popcorn at him. When the lights came up, we saw he was in a wheelchair—with a breathing tube sticking out of his neck. FML

Today I was walking down the street and saw a $20 bill on the ground. I thought it had fallen out of the pocket of the man in front of me, so I decided to do the right thing and ask him if he had dropped it. He said yes and took it. I later realized the $20 was mine. FML

Today I was singing Alicia Keys songs in the shower and hitting the insanely high notes. My father ran into the bathroom and threw open the shower door, shouting. He thought I was wailing in pain. FML

Today I had to run to catch my train, so I didn't get the chance to buy a ticket first. When the conductor was in sight, I noticed that he was a young man, so I opened my top a little, in the hope that I wouldn't have to pay. When I told him I hadn't bought a ticket, he said, "Close your top, I'm gay." FML

Today I got my first tattoo. It was a surprise for my fiancé: our names together over a heart. I went home, but before I could show him, he said we had to have a "talk." Now my ex's name is tattooed on my back. The kicker? I'm allergic to the ink. FML

Today I walked into my house to find everyone sitting around the table looking sad. I thought it would be a good time to crack a joke, so I said, "What's wrong? Grandma finally die?" She did. FML

Today, while I was out to lunch, my sister called me and asked me to pick her up from the mall. I told her she'd have to wait. She got pissed off and started cursing at me, so I hung up on her. She called me back thirty-seven times, so I finally answered and yelled, "WILL YOU LEAVE ME THE FUCK ALONE?" It was my boss. FML

Today I was supposed to look at an apartment. Thirty minutes after the time I was to meet the owner, she still hadn't shown up. I called her. When I got no response, I was annoyed and kept calling and calling, ready to scream at her. Finally she answered: "I'm in the hospital with my father. He just died. Please stop calling me." FML

Today my mother told me she didn't want my girlfriend spending the night anymore. I asked why, and she said she had heard us doing the nasty the night before. I denied it, hoping I could call her bluff. She paused for a moment and proceeded to moan *exactly* like my girlfriend. FML

Today I went for a walk with the guy I like. He held my hand, so I decided to tell him that I had feelings for him. He said that he had feelings for me, too. I smiled and leaned in to kiss him. He put his hand on my face and pushed it away, and said, "Until your acne clears, we are *not* together." FML

Today we watched a movie in class. Afterward, the professor asked us what we thought. I raised my hand and said it was pretentious, dull, and a really poor example of filmmaking. It was the movie he had spent five years writing and directing. FML

Today I saw two lovely ladies leave my neighbor's house, and a couple of minutes later he walked out. I made the international male "Did you fuck her/them" hand gesture—a horizontal fist pump. They were his daughters. FML

Today I was babysitting a seven-year-old girl, and we were eating chocolate-covered nuts. She kept on chewing the nuts and wondered where the chocolate was. I told her that to taste the chocolate, you had to suck on them. The first thing she told her parents when they got home was "I learned how to suck nuts!" FML

Today a guy informed me that the cute, really tiny leather bracelet with little silver hearts and several snaps that I'd found in a head shop is a cock ring. I'm a girl. FML

Today I was doing a striptease for
my husband. He asked me to stop. FML

Today I woke up at my grandparents' house. Still half asleep, I went to brush my teeth. Midbrush, my mouth started going numb. I inspected the toothpaste. It was my grandpa's anti-itch anal cream. FML

Today my best friend resolved things with her boyfriend after he had admitted to cheating. I felt really guilty because last month I had drunkenly hooked up with him. She told me, "I felt better when he told me that the girl was extremely ugly and bad in bed." FML

Today I was babysitting my co-worker's son. He was eating Jell-O and spilled it on his shirt, so I pulled off his pajamas and went into his room to grab a new pair. I heard a thump and ran to find him out cold on the floor. His parents walked in on me trying to wake up their naked three-year-old. FML

Today the kids I teach informed me that I had spelled my name incorrectly on the board. I looked at it and assured them that I had spelled it correctly. I'm twenty-two and a graduate student; they're six and mentally challenged. Guess who was right? FML

Today I bought a parakeet for my kids. When I got home and presented it to them, they wanted to let him fly around inside. We went around the house making sure all the windows and doors were shut. I forgot about the ceiling fan. FML

Today I interviewed for a full scholarship to college. During the interview, I said that I was excited about the new dean because I thought she'd be able to really make improvements and bring the school back to where it used to be. After the interview, I learned that my interviewer was the former dean. FML

Today a man on the train asked me if I had any change. I quickly responded, saying, *"No habla ingles."* He then tapped me on the shoulder and said, "That would've been a lot more believable if you weren't reading that English newspaper." FML

Today it took me over three hours to cut out little letters for an event I'm putting on. It took the wind less than a second to blow them all over campus. FML

Today my family and I were at a restaurant. We're Swedish, and we love talking about people in our language because no one here ever understands. I decided to comment about how ugly the girl at the next table was. She turned around and said, *"Dra åt helvete."* That's Swedish for "Go to hell." FML

Today my boss forgot her meeting with an official from the military base and called to ask me to handle it. The very cute Marine showed up that afternoon, and we talked for an hour. After he left, I realized I had forgotten about the paper mustache I had taped to my face as a joke this morning. FML

Today I went over to my uncle's house for dinner, and my stomach started to hurt really bad. I noticed there were two toilets, so I sat on the nicer one and proceeded to take a huge dump. It turned out that I had chosen the brand-new toilet. It hadn't been connected yet. FML

Today I went to get my midterm essay grade, thinking I couldn't have made lower than a B. I got an F. The professor wrote: "Best essay I read. Would've been an A if it had been the right topic." I had written about the Industrial Revolution instead of the Scientific Revolution. FML

Today I was eating lunch naked at my home, while watching porn on the big screen. I heard the garage door opening, meaning that my roommate was home. In my haste to get dressed, I fell back into the barstool I had been sitting on and knocked myself out. I woke up, naked, with lettuce all over me. FML

Today I was standing on a crowded bus, going home after school. A wriggling five-year-old boy and his mom left their seat to get off the bus. Since no one looked keen to sit there, I did, only to find out that it was covered in pee. FML

Today I was talking to my grandmother, who was lying down on the couch under a blanket, watching TV. As I was leaving, I said, "See you later, Nana," and patted her on the shoulder. Her shoulder was soft, and moved more than I had expected. It was her boob. I felt up my grandmother. FML

Today my mom was helping me unpack from college. She opened a box and took out some anal beads I had received as a gag gift. She asked, "What are these?" I answered, "They are for massaging your back." She then insisted that I show her. So I massaged my mother with anal beads. FML

Today I woke up to find that my car had been broken into. I was upset about not hearing my car alarm go off, until I realized that it *had* gone off in the middle of the night. I had woken up, cursed the idiot who had set off the alarm, put a pillow over my head, and fallen back to sleep. FML

Today my friends and I were drinking boba, a type of East Asian tea. On the side of the cup it said, "Please drink carefully to avoid choking on the boba." I started to laugh at the ridiculousness of the label and proceeded to choke on the boba in a coughing fit. FML

Today, when I was shaving, I wanted to see what I looked like with a Hitler mustache. Since I was shaving anyway, I just left that part and figured I'd shave it off later. I was messing around my room for a while, and then I forgot about it. Later that day, I ran into my girlfriend's parents. FML

Today I went for a jog in my neighborhood. While I was running, I passed my girlfriend's parents, who were out for a walk. Trying to make a good impression, I stopped to talk. When I got home, I realized I was wearing a shirt that friends had given me as a joke. It said: "Blow me, bitch. It's my b-day." FML

Today I babysat three-year-old twins.
They have a huge dry-erase board
hanging between their beds. After
they fell asleep, I was bored and
drew a very large, detailed penis
on the board. When I went to erase
it, I realized I had used a permanent
marker. FML

Today my child said to me, "Mommy, sometimes my peepee goes up like a stick." I said, "Well, honey, that's normal and okay." Then I asked when it does that. He replied, "Sometimes when I'm watching *Scooby-Doo* and Shaggy comes out dressed in lady clothes." FML

Today I met a really nice couple at a bar. We talked, and the conversation eventually drifted toward online dating. I casually commented that hooking up through the Internet was sad and pathetic. They had met on MySpace. FML

Today I was giving my boyfriend a hickey when I felt something squirt into my mouth. I had popped a pimple on his neck into my mouth. FML

Today I found an old dress lying around in my house. I decided to dye it green to wear on St. Patrick's Day. It turned out to be my grandmother's wedding dress, which my sister was planning to wear for her wedding. FML

Today I was out on a date with a guy. His hot co-worker came to have a beer with us, and I knew my best friend would think he was gorgeous. I wanted to take a picture of him without him knowing, so I tried holding up my phone and pretending to be texting. The flash went off. FML

Today I celebrated my sixteenth birthday. Thinking that my parents were at work, I decided it would be fun to tan nude in my backyard. My parents had set up a surprise sweet sixteen party for me. I stood naked in front of half my school. FML

Today my mother called me and told me that she had gone to the hospital. This wasn't a surprise because she normally goes to the hospital for the smallest things. So I was a smart-ass and asked, "What now? You finally have lung cancer from all those cigarettes?" She does. FML

Shit Out of Luck

For some people, ending up in the wrong place at
the wrong time seems to be an everyday occurrence.
We all get unlucky sometimes, but these people
seem to be contenders for the Murphy's Law awards.
"It's not my fault," they may whine, but sometimes
we can't help wondering if there's some kind of bad-
luck disease or if these people are just genetically
programmed to have shit happen to them. Then again,
tomorrow's another day. Or is it?

Today I waited two hours for my turn in the hospital. I was sitting next to an old lady with Alzheimer's disease who asked me forty-three times if I wanted a cookie. FML

Today it was my birthday. My girl-friend bought me a Nickelback CD. FML

Today I was the only one in an elevator when an attractive girl got in, talking on her phone. She told her friend, "I have to go; there's a cute guy on this elevator." Before I could even react, she turned to me and said, "Sorry for lying. I really wanted to get off the phone with her." FML

Today I was at a restaurant with a girl I like, and as I was getting my wallet out, I dropped a condom. She didn't see anything, and I waited to pick it up to avoid drawing atten-tion to it. The waiter walked past, picked it up, and held it out to me with a huge grin. FML

Shit Out of Luck

Today we got our school yearbooks. I opened to my profile to see that they had misspelled my first name, which is James. They had written "Lames." FML

Today I bought a fancy new electric razor. I tried it and then washed it out. I started to shake it dry. It was pretty slippery, and it exploded on the floor of my bathroom. The warranty doesn't cover this. FML

Today my tennis coach showed up to practice in an all-white outfit. I exclaimed, "You're looking very white today!" He's black. FML

Today I came home to find a puppy in my backyard. Thinking it was lost or a stray, I took it to the pound. My boyfriend came home and asked me if I had seen my present: the puppy. We went back to the pound to get it, but it had already been adopted. FML

Today I suggested that my mother download Skype so we could video chat while I'm studying in London over the summer. After I had explained how it worked and that it was free, she said, "Well, you'll only be gone for a few months. It's not really worth it." FML

Today, before a big formal banquet, I went to a tanning salon because I wanted to look good in my cocktail dress. I got out of the tanning bed, only to realize that I had left my socks on. FML

Today I was at the airport in India, where the men and women are searched separately. The guy welcoming us pointed me toward the women's area. It took me fifteen minutes to explain that I'm a guy. FML

Today I was cutting a bagel, only to slice the back of my hand with the knife. As I grabbed paper towels to clean up the blood, I noticed that the bagel had been presliced. FML

Today my wife, in her pristine wedding dress, got her period during the ceremony. How did I find out? The same way everyone else did. FML

Today, at seven in the morning, I ended up outside in a nightgown, barefoot, and in the rain. I found out that my two-year-old son now knows how to close the patio door, which, of course, has no outside door handle. FML

Today I drank a beer that I thought was mine. It wasn't. Someone had put out their cigarette in it. FML

Today I was trapped for forty minutes in L.A. traffic after a car overturned and all five lanes of the 101 S freeway were closed. When the traffic finally began to move, my car wouldn't start, because I'd left the headlights on and was listening to the radio. I was in the middle lane of the freeway. FML

F My Life

Today I was told that my mom and her new husband have named my newborn baby brother "Titan." FML

Today I went to a club, and my friends and I went up on the stage. A security guard told me to get down, saying that the stage was only for girls. I'm twenty-three, and I'm a girl. FML

Today I was carrying my mug of hot chocolate. When I got to the living room, my sleeve got caught on the door handle. FML

Today I crashed into a ditch on my way home from work. I had to walk two miles in subzero weather before I could pick up a cell phone signal to call a tow truck. When I got back to my car, a cop was waiting for me with a ticket for leaving the scene of an accident. FML

Today it's my birthday, but I had to go to work. I caught the train and was forced to sit next to this weird, smelly guy, who got off one stop before mine. A little old lady jumped on, so I scooted over to let her have enough room to sit down. Upon exiting the train, I noticed that my pants were wet with the guy's piss. FML

Today a girl was coming on to me and buying me drinks during a concert. At the end of the evening, she gave me her number so that we could go out. Because of the booze, I forgot it. FML

Today I danced with a girl until the bar closed. We went back to my place. She had a penis. FML

Today I went to the movies with a friend and her grandma. Her grandma was using toothpicks and carelessly dropping them on the ground. I took a big handful of popcorn from the bucket on the floor and got a piece of her toothpick lodged in my throat. FML

Today I decided to lighten my hair
color. I applied the dye and waited
twenty minutes. When I went to wash
the dye out, the water wouldn't turn
on. After my head started to burn,
I called the landlord in a panic.
There was a water main break and the
water was off for the entire city
block. FML

Today a ball rolled up to me, so I picked it up and threw it over the school wall. A little boy came up and asked for his ball back. It was Sunday, and the school was closed. FML

Today I fell flat on my ass while running for the subway, only to find out that the train had been standing by for ten minutes. I rode to work with a train full of people who had watched me fall. FML

Today I was on a date with a pretty girl. I attempted to put my arm around her, but elbowed her in the face instead. FML

Today I fell from the top of the stairs, caught myself in the middle, stood up, stepped down one more, tripped, and fell down the rest. FML

Today I left work and, because of the nice weather, decided to walk home across town. Only when I entered my apartment did I notice that the bottom of my miniskirt was tucked into my underwear. FML

Today I was standing on a desk at work changing a lightbulb, since we had no ladder. My phone rang, so I rushed to answer it, tripped, and smashed my leg. It was my boss, calling to tell me that he was bringing a ladder. FML

Today I was visiting my grandmother, and I overheard her having phone sex. FML

Today I was looking after my parents' house and their dog, and I fell asleep on the couch. The dog proceeded to climb onto my shoulders and rest behind my head like a doggie pillow. She farted right in my left ear. FML

Today I left with my boyfriend and his family on a trip to the tropics. When we got to the airport, security stopped me and opened my carry-on bag. I'd forgotten about the no-liquids rule. His whole family watched them take out bottles of lube, Vagisil, and Nair. FML

Today I farted in my cubicle, thinking no one would smell it. Two seconds later, everyone came to my cubicle to wish me a happy birthday. FML

Today I came home early from work and discovered my husband wearing a black babydoll nightdress, black stockings, and high heels. He says it helps him to relax. FML

Today I was having sex with a guy I had just met. I thought he was about to have an orgasm, but he was having an asthma attack. FML

Today I was walking in the snow and saw a kid slip and fall. I laughed and felt good about myself. Then *I* fell. FML

Today an airline lost my luggage when I was flying back from France. They had also lost my luggage when I flew *to* France. FML

Today I hooked up with this man for the first time. He took off his shirt and I saw that he had a chest full of black hair. His name was shaved into it. FML

Today a really hot guy walked into my office. Wanting to impress him, I picked up the phone and pretended to be making a huge business deal, talking loudly about big sums of money. I put the phone down and smiled seductively at him. He said, "Hi! I'm here to connect your phone lines." FML

Today I'm twenty, and I'm going bald. FML

Today I fell asleep. I felt something on my face. I batted it away. It was my hamster. It died from hitting the wall. FML

Today I was eating ice cream and I noticed some on my jeans, so I wiped it off with my finger and licked it. It was bird shit. FML

Today I decided to send my boyfriend a picture text of me naked. I accidentally sent it to my dad. He sent a text back, saying, "You definitely take after your mom." FML

Today I was awarding medals to finalists in a school club. While putting one around someone's neck, I ended up poking a girl in the eye. She tried to walk across the stage, but her eyes were watering. She missed the step and fell, breaking her ankle. FML

Today I took a picture from afar for my photography course. The shot was of a random adorable couple kissing in the snow. Later, upon closer inspection, I realized that the guy was my boyfriend. FML

Today I woke up to find my car covered in shaving cream and tampons and the word "CHEATER" written on my windshield in lipstick. The guy a few doors down from me has the same car as I do. I'm a virgin. FML

Today, while my four-year-old nephew was hugging me, he stepped back and declared, "Auntie, my pee-do is hard. Will it go away?" FML

Today, as I was walking my friend's
dog around the neighborhood, I
noticed a little girl fall off her
bike. I let go of the dog and ran
over to help. The girl was fine, but
the dog ran into the street and was
hit by a truck. FML

Today my boyfriend was really stressed about a guy he works with being a jerk. I told him, "If you ignore something long enough, it won't bother you anymore." He replied, "I've ignored my herpes for a long time, but it still bothers me." We've been having sex for three months. FML

Today I woke up at 5:00 and studied for my 9:30 exam for four hours. When I left my dorm at 9:00, it was dark outside. It turned out that I had slept through the entire day and woken up at 5:00 p.m. FML

Today, when I went to my car, I discovered an apologetic note on the windshield from the city telling me that they had hit my car. On top of that note was a parking ticket, also from the city. FML

Today my friend was picking on me at school by constantly tapping on my shoulder. At recess, I had had enough. I felt the familiar tap on my shoulder, and I drove my elbow into his stomach. It was the principal. FML

Today I bit into my egg sandwich, and when I looked at it, there were five long gray hairs leading from the sandwich into my mouth. FML

Today I found out that I am being sued for losing a set of wedding photos that I had taken. I had lost them by being mugged on the way home from the shoot and having $10,000 worth of equipment stolen from me. FML

Today I wanted to seduce my boyfriend, so I put on my sexiest lingerie and started playing mood music. As he was eating dinner, I climbed up on the table and started seductively crawling across to him. The table collapsed. FML

Today my tattoo artist boyfriend of five months gave me my first tattoo in celebration of my eighteenth birthday. It was supposed to be a heart with my name in script. He had spelled my name wrong. FML

Today I had to call my mom and tell
her about the insurance claim that is
going to be coming through in the next
couple of weeks because I had spent a
night in the hospital. I'm allergic to
vaginal lube. FML

Today, while I was working at my cash register, a well-
dressed man who was six foot three came in and ordered.
After he ordered I asked why he was dressed so nicely. He
responded, "I'm going to court for stalking pretty girls like
you." Our name tags have our full names. FML

Today my friend had a Coke can on his desk in class. It was
empty, but I was thirsty, so I picked it up, thinking I could try to
get that little bit of Coke that is always left at the bottom. When
I took a sip, I found that he had been picking his fingernails and
putting them in the can. FML

Today I had to tell my super-conservative parents that I had
just gone to visit the boyfriend I'm not supposed to have so I
could tell him that I am pregnant. FML

Today my grandma was showing me an ancient family letter. Apparently it had been written by a famous historical figure. She was going on about how important it was, that it was in such good condition, and that it was worth a lot. I dropped my glass of juice. It spilled all over the letter. FML

Today I dropped my $400 iPhone, which has survived toilets and six-foot falls, on a Walmart floor, shattering the screen. I did manage, however, to catch the $2 box of macaroni and cheese before it hit the ground. FML

Today I walked into my room to find that my mom had made my bed and done my laundry, for which I thanked her with a hug. I lay down on the bed, stretched out my arms, and realized that my vibrator was still under the pillow where I had left it. FML

Today my first real date ended with the girl saying, "Thanks for dinner. I was hungry—and, oh, by the way, I'm a lesbian." FML

Today I was looking after a hamster for a friend. My dog ate it. FML

Today, as I was texting with a girl I've been trying to hook up with, she complained about how crummy a day she was having. I told her that it couldn't be as bad as she thought and she would probably get over it soon. Then she told me she had found out that her cousin had been murdered. FML

Today I went to get my blood drawn for the first time. After I explained to the nurse how nervous I was, she replied, "Oh honey, don't worry! This is my first time too!" FML

Today the hard drive on my computer crashed with all of my files on it. I took it to my dad, who is a computer analyst, to see if he could recover anything. The only thing that he could salvage was my illustrious collection of porn. FML

Today I was presenting in PowerPoint.
I plugged in the cord that connected
my computer to the projector, forget-
ting what my boyfriend had set as my
desktop picture the night before. I
opened my laptop, and projected on the
wall was a picture of me in the nude.
I go to Catholic school. FML

Today my girlfriend came up behind me and put her hands in
my back pockets. I thought it was someone trying to take my
wallet, so I elbowed her in the nose and broke it. FML

Today I left my glasses at home. While walking to the bus stop, I
saw the cutest girl on the block smiling and waving at me from
her front yard. I happily waved back, smiling, and kept going. It
turned out that she was crying and calling me over. Her dad had
just had a heart attack. FML

Today I took my dog for a walk down by the river. I was
throwing sticks for him with one hand and talking on the
phone with the other. Then realized that I had thrown my
phone into the river and was standing there talking to the
stick. FML

Today I was volunteering at a
nursing home, and I was calling
bingo numbers. One woman stood up
and started making noises. I assumed
she had won, and I started clapping.
She fell on the floor and died of a
heart attack. I had applauded her
death. FML

missbean

Today, while I was working, my ex-girlfriend came in to apply for a job. She had broken up with me for another guy, so I can't stand being in the same room with her. The manager hired her on the spot. I have to train her. FML

Today a customer I've been waiting on for years came into the restaurant after a long absence. I said to him, "Hey, man, it looks like you lost a lot of weight! How'd you do it?" He replied, "I got cancer." FML

Today I was working at Chuck E. Cheese's. I had to put on the mouse costume. Due to the disgusting smell in the costume and how hot it was to wear, I fainted in front of all the people at a birthday party. I awoke to see a little boy screaming. He then proceeded to kick me in the face and run. FML

Today my boyfriend and I discreetly ordered sex toys online and had them delivered to my dorm room. They were sent to the billing address. It's my parents' credit card. FML

Today I was eating nacho chips with my nieces, and I found that some were wet. I looked at my niece and noticed that she was sucking on the chips and putting them back in the bag. FML

Today I borrowed a van to move some of my furniture. I wasn't used to the brakes, so when I stopped at a red light, I pretty much ended up in the crosswalk. Suddenly I heard a loud thud at the side of the van. I turned to find out what kind of idiot would walk into a van. It was a blind man. FML

Today I hit a car while trying to answer a phone call. Frustrated, I quickly answered the phone and shouted, *"What?!"* To which my mom replied, "I just had a bad feeling in my gut about you, so I wanted to make sure you were okay." FML

Today my family gathered at my ninety-six-year-old great-grand-mother's surprise birthday party, which was my idea. When she walked in, we surprised her so much that she had a heart attack. She is now in the hospital. FML

Today, two days before my birthday, my parents drove three hours to visit me at school and take me out to lunch. I assumed that it was to celebrate my birthday. They told me they are getting divorced. FML

Today I was sleeping because I had been sick. The closest bathroom to mine is the one in my parents' room. I woke up and felt like I had to throw up, so I ran into my parents' room to go to the bathroom. I walked in on my parents having sex. Shocked, I gasped for air and threw up all over their bed. FML

Today I was at the beach with my buddy. Messing around, he swam up behind me and dunked me under the water. Naturally, moments later I swam behind him, grabbed both his ankles, and stood up, flipping him completely . . . only to see him watching me from a few feet away. I had flipped a seventy-year-old man. FML

Today my mom bought me a T-shirt. It has the U.S. Marines logo on it and says "Marine's Girlfriend." I'm a straight sixteen-year-old boy. My mom reads and speaks only Spanish. FML

Today I realized that my roommate has been using my loofah to clean our toilet. I've been cleaning myself with the shit of four college boys for the last six months. FML

Today I laced up my fabulous new boots and walked outside to find my hot neighbor, with whom I carpool every morning. Feeling quite confident, I struck a pose. Upon taking my first step down the stairs, I fell forward. I woke up hours later with seven stitches in my head. FML

Today I was in the changing room at the local YMCA. I went to use the hair dryer but couldn't because a naked old man was bent over, butt cheeks spread wide with his hands and ass aimed at the dryer. He was enjoying it. FML

Today I was getting my teeth cleaned at the dentist's office. Looking up at his nose, I saw runny snot dripping onto his lip. I tried to slowly move away. "Stop!" he ordered me. The movement of his lips caused the snot to fall right into my mouth. FML

Today I went to the ER for severe pain in my abdominal area. The doctor came in after looking at the CAT scan and said, "Well, it's not your appendix." Thinking I was in the clear, I said, "That's awesome." The doctor responded, "It's probably your testicles." FML

Today I overheard my parents having sex. Trying to be the reasonable person I am, I dismissed it, realizing that sex is just normal. I was walking quickly past their bedroom when my cat ran past me into the room, cracking open the door. My parents think I was peeping and need therapy. FML

Today I was working at ▇rget when an elderly woman asked me if I could help her find her favorite bra. I proceeded to ask what brand it was. She replied, "I'll check the tag." She lifted up the front of her shirt and flipped one cup of her bra inside out. I saw everything. FML

Today I went for a job interview on my birthday. I had on a shirt and a tie, and I had my BlackBerry in my pocket. I was running a little late, so I dashed outside. As I went out the door, a bunch of my buddies screamed "HAPPY BIRTHDAY!" and poured Gatorade all over me. FML

Today I was going to a Harry Potter convention, since I love the books so much. On the drive there, I got lost, and it only got worse when my car broke down. Since I had forgotten my cell phone, I decided to try to hitch a ride. I stood on the side of the road for two hours dressed like Ron Weasley. FML

Today I scored the winning goal in the state finals. For the other team. FML

Today I was meeting my sister's fiancé. I stopped at an Internet café on the way to her house for dinner. I was sitting at a computer, and there was a really attractive man next to me. We flirted and exchanged numbers. It turned out that he was my sister's fiancé. FML

Today I was at this awesome party, and I was dancing with a really attractive girl, who suddenly started making out with me. Five minutes later, my friend told me that the girl had just given him a blow job. FML

Today I drove my girlfriend home
around 11:00 p.m. When we got to her
garage, we started to have sex. When
she began to climax, she slipped and
hit her head. Her parents heard the
crash and came downstairs. We were
both naked. She was unconscious. FML

missbean

Today I came home early from work to surprise my son with a new mountain bike for his birthday. To keep it a surprise, I carried it quietly up to his bedroom. As I opened the door, I heard my son say, "Oh, man, you're gonna make me come," to the girl he was on top of. He just turned fourteen. FML

Today I decided to do a load of laundry. A minute into the cycle, as the water started to drip into the machine, I realized that I had left my iPod in my sweatpants pocket. The washing machine door locks automatically and cannot be opened until the forty-minute cycle is up. FML

Today I had a job interview. I stopped to take a pee in the lobby before I went in. I relaxed a bit too much at the urinal and accidentally farted. I proceeded to chuckle about it like a five-year-old for a few seconds. The guy next to me at the urinal turned out to be the interviewer. FML

Today I woke up to find that the large container of leftover beef stroganoff that I had put down the garbage disposal last night had backed up into my bathtub. FML

Today I was arrested because my six-year-old son called the police, saying that I was hitting my wife and that she was crying. My wife and I had been having sex. FML

Today I was taking the subway to school. It was about 6:30 a.m., and I was listening to music and catching up on some homework. I took my headphones off for a second to adjust them. While they were off, I heard some grunting and looked over at the man across from me. He was masturbating. FML

Today my mom brought my dog in to wake me up. He jumped up on the bed. I started to pet what I thought was his neck and played with a random tuft of fur. I soon realized that it was his penis. FML

Today I went out on my porch for a late-night cigarette. Then I opened the door and took one step back inside, and all I remember is a big thud. I woke up five minutes later to see my father standing over me and saying, "Nice right hook, huh?" Then he chuckled. He had thought I was a burglar, so he knocked me out. FML

Today I was sitting in math class, and
I glanced over to the other side of
the room, where the hottest girl in
the school was sitting. I could see
her thong, so I instantly got a boner.
About a minute later my teacher called
me up to the board to do a problem. I
had worn basketball shorts that day.
FML

Today I tried to prove to my dad that he snores by secretly putting a tape recorder under his bed. I soon found out that my
parents had had sex that night. My mom likes to talk dirty. FML

Today my mom came to me and asked if I had drunk her wine.
I'm sixteen, so I lied and said no. The next morning there was a
tape on my bed labeled "Pool house security cameras —Love,
Mom." It was a video of me downing her red wine and having
sex with my boyfriend. FML

Today, on the train home, a gun was placed against the back
of my head and my wallet, watch, and iPod were stolen. As
soon as the robber got what he wanted, he turned and ran,
dropping his weapon to the ground. I had been mugged with
a PEZ dispenser. FML

Today I was watching a movie with my boyfriend and his parents. An intense sex scene came on. I felt grateful when I saw his father reaching for the remote to fast-forward through the scene. Instead, he put it into slow motion. We watched in silence for about three minutes before he managed to fix it. FML

Today I was woken up by the sound of power tools at 6:30 a.m. I stuck my head out the window and yelled at them to shut up. They didn't stop. I walked out the front door to find the bastard. It was firemen. They were sawing down the door of my neighbor's burning house. FML

Today I was on the subway. I have fairly serious obsessive-compulsive disorder, so I avoid holding on to the poles or handles. All the seats were taken, so I leaned against a wall. At the next stop, an obese, sweaty man got on and grabbed the two poles on either side of me, effectively hugging me. My shirt was wet when he left. FML

Today I checked my Facebook page to find that I had been tagged in a bunch of photos from a party I had attended last night. On each picture was a comment from my mom saying "You're grounded." FML

Today I was curling my eyelashes
in the bathroom when my brother
flung open the door. I jumped up,
startled, and ended up ripping out
all my eyelashes. I now have to
wait until they grow back. FML

missbean

Today I texted my boyfriend to tell him how terrible I felt about cheating. He replied, saying he was so relieved because he had been cheating on me with a girl in his dorm. I was talking about my math exam. FML

Today my phone rang while I was home alone. When I picked up, all I could hear was heavy breathing. Convinced it was one of my friends playing a joke, I said loudly, "Get off the phone, you fucker, and don't call back!" It turned out it was my grandma. She was having a stroke. FML

Rock Bottom

There are quite a few examples of world-class victims. We can sneer at their predicaments, but we can also take pity on them. And then laugh some more. The good news is that in one short sentence they are able to get straight to the heart of the problem, thus saving thousands of dollars in therapist's fees. We can choose to offer them assistance in the form of a helping hand . . . or perhaps even a swift kick in the rear. But most often, a little kindness should suffice. They deserve at least that much for their honesty, right?

Today I realized that the dog humping my leg was the most action I've gotten in months. FML

Today I was talking to my friend about my life and she stopped me midsentence to tell me that my life makes her sad. FML

Today I signed up for an online dating site. After completing the personality quiz, I set the distance to a sixty-mile radius around where I live. Then I set it to the country. Then to the whole world. I got no matches for any of the settings. FML

Today I got an email from the local Dungeons & Dragons meet-up group that the next meeting will be on February 14. I don't know what is more sad: that the group is meeting on Valentine's Day or that I have nothing better to do than go. FML

Today it's my birthday. It's 6:30 p.m., and I'm still the only person aware of what day it is. FML

Today I organized a romantic evening with one of my old squeezes, hoping that I could reignite something special. She showed up at 8:00 and told me that she had to leave by 9:00. She was gone by 8:30. FML

Today I'm twenty years old and have never been kissed. FML

Today I got an email from a guy I'd had a one-night stand with. He wanted to get together to talk about it. It turned out that he was in rehab and wanted to address the biggest mistakes he'd ever made in his life. I am on that list of regrets. FML

Today I was so lethargic at work that the light in my office, which comes on when triggered by a motion detector, went off. FML

Today I found out that my best friends went on a crazy party weekend and they didn't invite me. FML

Today I sat next to a hot babe. I was feeling nervous. Nevertheless, I managed to shyly ask for her phone number. It was the first time I'd ever done this. Only when I arrived back home did I realize that there was a digit missing. FML

Today I met the girl who had dumped me because the distance between us was too great. We're in the same city again. She's now dating a Marine stationed in Iraq. FML

Today I yelled while I was sleeping. I was sleeping during a very important meeting with all the customers and my boss. FML

Today I kissed the girl I love for the first time. Her reaction? She threw up. FML

Today, because I'm a French girl in England, a cute boy asked me where I live exactly. When I told him Paris, he answered, "Strange, I always heard Parisians were the most beautiful women in the world." FML

Today I went to have a drink with my friend. On the way I withdrew twenty bucks from an ATM, and when I arrived at the bar I realized I had taken my card from the machine, but not the twenty. FML

Today I discovered that there is a security camera in the storage room where I work—the same room where, two days ago, I had masturbated. FML

Today my boss sneezed onto his hands, then licked them in front of my best customers. FML

Today I pointed out to my girlfriend that she isn't jealous. She replied, "Well, actually, I am. I just can't prove it because no one else is interested in you." FML

Today I helped my son do his math homework. He got a C and won't talk to me anymore. FML

Today it's my birthday. Before my girlfriend gave me the present she had bought for me, I jokingly said, "I hope it's not a tie!" It was. FML

Today my fourteen-year-old little sister asked me how I had felt when I had my first sexual experience. I told her it was personal and was none of her business. Then she looked at me and said, "I thought it was nice." I'm nineteen and a virgin. FML

Today my girlfriend came home with new condoms: Extended Pleasure, containing a numbing gel designed to help me last longer. FML

Today, while doing it with my girlfriend, she asked, "Will you be done anytime soon?" FML

Today my mom took me to the doctor for my annual physical. Puberty still hasn't arrived, and the doctor seemed concerned. He left the room, leaving the door ajar. I overheard him discussing my undeveloped penis with my mom, and then he brought her in to show her "the problem." FML

Today I asked my girlfriend if she wanted to go to the movies. She replied, "Sorry, I have to do stuff with my parents." Her mom called, and by mistake my girlfriend hit the speakerphone. The first thing her mom said was "Be back at eleven." FML

Today at 2:23 a.m., my drunken girlfriend called me from a party, where she was the only girl. She seemed to be having a great time. FML

Today my girlfriend made fun of me, saying that I'm too emotional. This really pissed me off, and I started shouting at her to show her that I'm "all man," which made me start crying. FML

Today I aimed at the little blue disk placed at the bottom of the urinal. I learned the hard way that when the pee splashes off, it makes little blue stains on pants. FML

Today someone I used to know got in touch with me, after I hadn't heard from him in years. He insisted that we meet up as soon as possible and wanted me to go to his house that afternoon. I spent the afternoon repairing his computer, and I haven't heard from him since. FML

Today I went to a speed-dating evening. After seven minutes, the girl told me she wasn't interested. I asked her at what point of the conversation she had made up her mind, and she answered, "When you said 'Hello.' Goodbye." FML

Today I turned around in my cubicle to see my whole department getting ready to have lunch together. Nobody had mentioned it to me. FML

Today I got a letter of acceptance from Princeton. I jumped for joy, screaming at the top of my lungs. My little brother walked in with his camcorder, laughing, and handed me the real letter. I had been turned down. FML

Today I went out to lunch with two
friends from high school. We saw a
girl that we had graduated with at the
restaurant. The girl gave both of them
hugs and introduced herself to me. FML

Today I just found out that the co-worker I had refused to
leave my wife for is now happily married to someone else. I'm
now divorced. FML

Today, though I'm normally unperturbed by my single status, I
walked by some squirrels engaged in mating rituals and felt a
pang of jealousy. FML

Today I told my boyfriend that I don't like his facial hair and
that he should shave it off. He replied, "You first." FML

Today I realized that I regret that break my ex and I took. I thought it would lead him to stop flirting and cheating with other girls and be with only me forever. Now I'm the girl he cheats on his girlfriend with. FML

Today I saw a friend in the street, but he didn't see me, so as a joke I decided to call him. He took his cell phone out of his pocket, sighed, and ignored it. FML

Today my boyfriend told me I smell like vegetables. FML

Today my mom asked all the old ladies in her church to pray that I meet "someone special." FML

Today I was trying to finish an English assignment but was not sure how to complete it. So I emailed my teacher to ask her, and she responded, "Flip over the handout for instructions." FML

Today the only cute girl in my office made fun of me because I'm twenty-seven and bring fruit cups with my lunch. FML

Today I daringly tried that fish bath treatment--where the fish come to you and eat all of your skin's dead cells. I submerged myself in it, and after fifteen minutes of my being their human buffet, twenty of the fish died. FML

Today I told the man I love to "go first" when we started talking at the same time. I wanted to confess my feelings; he wanted to tell me about his engagement. FML

Today I realized that I've been dating a girl for a year, and she's only touched my penis twice. Once was by accident. FML

Today my brother's girlfriend dumped him. I overheard my mom tell him, "It could be worse. Your brother can't even get a girlfriend." FML

Today I realized that I know more about the Transformers' history than I do about talking to women. FML

Today I went to Target to buy some soap, and a seventy-year-old woman next to me was asking a sales associate if they had any bubble bath mix. I suddenly pictured her naked, bathing herself, and my dick just couldn't stay still. I haven't had sex in almost two years. FML

Today my girlfriend dumped me,
proclaiming that she wanted someone
more like her "Edward." I asked
her who Edward was. She held up a
copy of her *Twilight* book. She was
talking about a fictional vampire.
FML

missbean

Today I sent a Facebook friend request to my ex. This afternoon I
noticed that she had accepted and left a message for me in my
inbox . . . asking how she knew me. FML

```
Today I had to walk home from school
in the rain because my mom claimed
she didn't have a car to pick me up
in. When I got home, there was a car
in the driveway. FML
```

Today I am contemplating ending my relationship of six years. My
boyfriend is too busy playing Guitar Hero to listen. FML

Today I made a Craigslist ad looking for hot and horny
women who wanted some. I got only one reply, from another guy asking me if this kind of thing actually works.
FML

Today, just before I was going to end a thing I had with this guy, he beat me to it. It turned out that he had gotten back together with his ex-girlfriend and was just using me as a backup. FML.

Today I sneezed so hard I herniated my back. After passing out from the pain, I awoke on the floor, covered in my own shit and piss. Unable to move, I had to wait in this state for four hours until my wife returned home from work, cleaned me up, and took me to the hospital. FML

Today my dad learned how to use parental controls. I now have an 11:00 curfew. I am seventeen. FML

Today I hid my credit card from myself so I wouldn't use it. Now I can't find it. FML

Today I was on the phone with my
boyfriend for over an hour, listening
to him talk about his new truck and
his final exams. I literally did not
say one word. I finally got the chance
to say, "Hey, baby, guess what happened to me today?" He replied, "Can I
go to sleep? I'm too tired to guess.
Good night." And he hung up. FML

Today I gathered the courage to participate in a class discussion. My professor laughed at me. FML

Today I woke up at 5:15 a.m., shoveled and salted the driveway
for over an hour, left early, and drove an hour on shitty roads to
get to work on time, only to be laid off. FML

Today, on my eighteenth birthday, my mom told me that the
man I had thought was my father for my whole life was actually not my father. My real father is in prison for murder. FML

Today I went to the office and told my boss that I hated my job and was quitting. I tried to rush out, but I slipped and fell on the marble floor in front of the whole office. FML

Today the girl I have had a crush on for two years snuck up from behind me to give me a hug. I farted very loudly at the same exact moment. FML

Today I was offered a job. It took me only a year and seventeen interviews to get an offer. I have a PhD. FML

Today I remembered that I bought thirty condoms last year. I now have twenty-nine. FML

Today I was with the guy I am seeing, and we were fooling around in my room. I proposed sex. He said he didn't have time because he had to go play Mario Kart. FML

Today I hung out with my crush at his apartment for only the second time. He was having a party. After a few sips of my green apple Smirnoff, I puked up the Chinese food I had eaten earlier all over his new couch in front of him and a bunch of strangers. FML

Today I masturbated three times to the thought of my wife because we don't have sex anymore. FML

Today I had a wet dream. When I woke up, I was touching myself. I also woke up to find that I had fallen asleep on the couch after eating too much turkey at a family reunion. Twenty relatives were giving me nasty looks. FML

Today I asked a guy out on a coffee date, and we started talking about our mutual careers. At the end of the date, he asked me if I had any more questions about job opportunities or any more advice, then shook my hand and gave me his card. FML

Today my fiancé told me that he no longer loves me, that he still has feelings for an ex. The wedding is off, and he needs the ring back to give to the right woman. FML

Today my four-year-old niece asked me why I didn't have a job or a wife. FML

Today I was singing to my cat, and she reached up and put her paw over my mouth. FML

Today my father asked me if he could
borrow my electric razor because
he wanted to "surprise Mom later."
Anxious to see him without his
lifelong beard, I willingly agreed.
Half an hour later he exited the
bathroom, beard fully intact. FML

Today I listened to my roommate having sex from 3:00 until 6:00 a.m. When I looked over at my girlfriend, who must have thought I was sleeping, I noticed that she was masturbating. FML

Today, for the first time ever, I saw a vagina in person. It was during med school training on how to do a pelvic exam. FML

Today, at the elementary school where I teach, the kids all voted for their favorite teacher. I was the only one to receive zero votes. When I asked a small group of students why no one had voted for me, one boy replied, "Because you're the ugliest." FML

Today I was going down on a girl. When I looked up, she was texting. FML

Today my phone rang for the first time in four days. It was my mom. She had dialed the wrong number. FML

Today I discovered a drawer in my house that was full of chocolates, cookies, and baked goods. When I asked my sister what the drawer was for, she told me that my mom thought it would be a good idea to hide the fattening foods from me. My entire family knew about the food drawer except me. FML

Today I woke up around 5:00 a.m. after a party I had given last night. I was still quite drunk. This chick from the night before was lying next to me. I kissed her, and about a minute and a half into some heavy making out she opened her eyes and said, "Oh, it's you." Then she got up and walked out. FML

Today, having just told me what a great job I've been doing and how he'd really like to start giving me some more responsibility, my boss asked me if I'd sharpen a couple of pencils for him. FML

Today I am finally dating the girl
I have liked on and off for the past
year. In the school play. FML

Today I cut myself with childproof scissors. FML

Today a flight attendant asked me if I was airsick, because I
looked really pale. I told her that that was my normal complex-
ion but thanked her for her concern. She insisted, "No, that
can't be normal." FML

Today I couldn't decide what was worse, my mom walking in
on me pleasuring myself or the one-hour talk about how it's
perfectly normal and even she does it. FML

Today my sister teased me about being a mistake. When I told my mom what my sister had said, her response was "I still love you anyway." FML

Today I made a joke about my wedding to my mom, and she told me not to joke about something that will probably never happen. FML

Today I finally reunited with old friends from school. It was great to see everyone all grown up and hear their stories. Before leaving, we decided to have a group photo for old times' sake. They asked me to take the picture. FML

Today I received my passport in the mail. They got my birth date wrong. Then I picked up my birth certificate, which I had sent in with the application. It turned out that my parents have been celebrating my birthday on the wrong day for sixteen years. FML

Today I found dark hairs growing on
my chest, nipples, and stomach. I'm
a nineteen-year-old girl. FML

Today I was giving my boyfriend a blow job. He was twitching and moving around and saying, "Oh yeah"; then he said, "Take that, bitch." I looked up to see that he was only excited about how he was dominating in Call of Duty 4. FML

Today I submitted my picture to a rating website. It was rejected because I didn't clarify which person I was. The picture was of my dog and me. FML

Today I took a friend out for what I thought was a date. After dinner was over and I had paid, she pulled the bill out and wrote her name and phone number on it for the waiter. FML

Today my girlfriend and I were watching a show about sex on the Discovery channel. The topic of female orgasms came up, and she said, "Wow, I wonder what that's like?" We've been sexually active for three years. FML

Today I was complaining to my mom about how my sister looked like a Barbie doll next to me. I was saying how she was so tan and her hair looked great compared to mine. My mom paused for a while and then said, "Well, you're pretty on the inside." FML

Today I was having sex for the first time with a girl I really like. After a while I told her I was about to come. She replied, "Lucky you." FML

Today I was happy because I heard my exact shirt and sweater were in *Seventeen* magazine. They were in the "what not to wear" category. FML

Today I told my college friend that I considered her to be my best friend. She responded, "I don't think you should call me that." FML

F My Life

Today, the ninth-grade dean called me in to his office to talk. He asked me if I was new because it seemed like I was having trouble making friends. I've been going to the same school, with the same people, since kindergarten. FML

Today, at the end of a really long day, my boyfriend was rubbing my back. I told him I appreciated how sensitive he was being. His response? "I was just trying to figure out how to unhook your bra." FML

Today I realized that my life is so boring that I could not think of a single thing to complain about. FML

Today I got fired from a great babysitting job because the little girl said I was boring. FML

Today I was watching a documentary about the world's fattest man. Halfway through the show, the reporter started talking about the guy's girlfriend. The fattest man in the world has a girlfriend. I'm twenty-one and have never had a girlfriend. FML

Today I was walking home from work, and a woman asked me to come inside for a free meal. It was at a homeless shelter. FML

Today I found out that my boyfriend owns and wears more thongs than I do. FML

Today I got my fake ID and went out with the boys to dinner and the bars. One of my friends asked to see my ID. He noticed that according to the birth date on it I wasn't over twenty-one. I had paid $170 for a fake ID with my real birth date. FML

Today my boyfriend fell asleep
during phone sex. FML

Today I asked to borrow my fat friend's pants for a semiformal tomorrow. I figured I'd just get a belt to hold the pants up. The pants fit me. FML

Today I realized that there are more framed pictures of my mom's dog than pictures of me around the house. FML

Today my boyfriend broke up with me. I cried and told him that I loved him. He gave me a quarter and told me to call someone who cared. I threw the quarter in his face and ran. I waited for the bus, but when I got on, I realized I was twenty-five cents short of the fare. I walked home in the rain. FML

Today my boyfriend gave me a card for my birthday and told me to open it ten minutes after he'd left. I waited five minutes. Inside the card it said, "It's not working out, but here's twenty bucks." FML

Today a girl I really like mentioned that she was home alone and that she was really, *really* lonely. She asked if I wanted to come over and watch a few movies with her. As I prepared to leave, she sent me a text saying, "Can you pick up my friend Spencer?" FML

Today I found out that my ex-girlfriend put Nair in my shampoo before moving out. I'm now bald. FML

Today I went to the doctor, and the nurse asked if I was married, to which I responded "yes." She then asked if I was sexually active. My response: "No." FML

Today my mom walked in on me while I was looking at a 1978 copy of *Playboy*. She asked if I had found it in the basement. I said yes. Then I realized that she was the centerfold. FML

Today I told a girl I liked her. She replied, "Don't." FML

Today my boyfriend asked me what I had enjoyed most about the weekend we'd spent together. I mentioned in detail a certain move he had pulled during sex. When asked what he enjoyed most, he replied, "Putting my fish tank together." FML

Today I was walking along the street and passed a young couple. Over my shoulder I heard the girl say to her boyfriend, "Would you still love me if I looked like her?" FML

Today my name was called during an assembly because I had won a prize. Everyone booed. FML

Today I was sitting in class, and I fell asleep during the lesson. I was wearing sweatpants and had an erection. My teacher came up to me and grabbed my penis. She thought it was my phone. FML

Today I was walking to my car when I saw a large man walking behind me. I hurried to open my car door as he quickly approached. My door wasn't unlocking, and I panicked. It was then that I noticed that it wasn't even my car. As I walked away from that car, he walked up and unlocked the door of it. FML

Today a creepy man on the subway said he liked my eyeballs. It was the best compliment I've received in months. FML

Today the local newspaper ran a story called "Looking Good," about fashion in school. The front page of that section featured a picture of my class. I was Photoshopped out. FML

Today I opened a birthday present from my grandfather. It was a map of the United States color-coded to show the regional percentage of available men. FML

Today my daughter asked me when was the first time I had had sex. When I told her it was at age twenty-two, she quickly shouted, "Beat ya!" She's thirteen. FML

Today I dropped my keys. Not wanting to lean over and pick them up, I pointed at them and said "*Accio*." I had tried to use a Harry Potter spell in public. FML

Today I had my final meeting with the psychologist who was helping me with my bipolar disorder. I just found out that he committed suicide. FML

Today I put my picture on a celebrity look-alike website. The three matches that came up were Barbra Streisand, Hillary Clinton, and Boy George. I'm sixteen. I'm a boy. FML

Today I was sitting in science class, and to my surprise I felt my pants suddenly becoming warm and wet. I looked behind me to see that four boys from my class had inserted a small funnel into my exposed butt crack and poured the melted butter from the experiment into it. FML

Today my cat was in the bathroom with me. I was getting undressed to get into the shower. My cat looked at me after I undressed and then proceeded to throw up all over the rug. FML

Today I was excited because I was going to get my college decisions back. I put all of the letters in order of my preference. Didn't get into my first choice. Denied by my second choice. Rejected by my third choice. Wait-listed on my backup choice. Accepted for a job at Target. FML

Today I was masturbating into a sock when I felt something on my cock. I quickly ripped the sock off and threw it on the floor. A huge spider came scurrying out. FML

Today I was diagnosed with pancreatic cancer. I called all my family members to invite them over this evening, telling them that I had some very important news for them that could not wait. They all declined the invite. When I asked why, they said they were going to my cousin's house to watch his new TV. FML

Today, after taking a shower, I decided to weigh myself. I peered down. I couldn't see the scale. FML

Today I decided to introduce my girlfriend to my parents by telling them that we were going to have a very special guest for dinner. While my mom was preparing the meal, she asked, "What does he like?" I'm straight. My parents thought differently. FML

The Banes of
Our Existence

When we come across someone mean, cynical, or just plain evil, there's nothing much to laugh about (well, maybe a little). Some people are just bad, and the worst are those few who don't know it. Let us now lower these miserable pieces of human waste into the smoldering embers of hell and bid them good riddance, for these are the people who make our lives a regular nightmare.

Today I got in line at the grocery store. The woman in front of me looked right at me, turned to her friend, and said, "That reminds me, I forgot to get acne cream." FML

Today I was on a train, sitting next to an old man who was reading a newspaper. Suddenly he sneezed without putting his hands over his nose. Instead of turning toward the window first, he turned toward me. FML

Today, during dinner, my new girlfriend's father stroked my leg several times under the table with his bare foot. FML

Today I was discussing my family heritage with my girlfriend's parents. The minute I told them I come from a German background, her seven-year-old brother pointed at me and yelled, "Hitler!" FML

Today it's my birthday. My ex just sent me a text. I read it, happy he had remembered. He wanted me to know he has a new girlfriend. FML

Today I got my license renewed, and the woman behind the desk looked at me and said, "Guess we need to update the weight, huh?" FML

Today I was reading the end of my book. I turned the page and saw, written at the top: "Lauren kills Paul in the end. You shouldn't have pissed me off." It was from my sister. We had a fight yesterday. FML

Today I sent a text message to my ex-boyfriend, who dumped me four months ago, telling him to come back. His answer: "Feeling-wise, I won't come back to you, but sexually, why not?" FML

Today my fiancé told me that, after seven years together, he is no longer in love with me. Shocked and appalled, I ask him if he had anything else to add. "Happy Birthday," he said. FML

Today my best friend invited me to dinner at his house. When I went to the bathroom, I found my wife's wedding ring in a cup. She lost it a week ago. FML

Today my boss called me in to tell me I was getting a raise. Excited, I bought a $1,500 Chanel bag. Two hours later he called me in to tell me that he had been kidding. FML

Today I decided to come out to a co-worker. She looked at me, laughed, and said, "You can't be gay, you're fat!" FML

Today, as I was taking the train to work with the worst hangover ever, two obese women started talking about rim jobs. I got up to change cars just in time for their conversation to switch to *receiving* rim jobs. I sprayed puke all over myself and an innocent bystander. FML

Today my boss told me that we are having a big meeting tomorrow, with lots of important people. Before leaving the room he added, "Please try to dress better tomorrow." FML

Today kids were chatting while I was trying to teach a lesson. After three warnings that the next person who talked would get a note to take home, one kid looked right at me and went, "Meeow." FML

Today at lunch I ordered a Coke. The waiter replied, "Diet Coke?" I corrected him, saying, "No, regular Coke." He shook his head and said again, "Diet Coke." FML

Today a woman at the crowded mall stopped me and told me loudly that if I bought her product it would get rid of my acne. FML

Today I was putting in a new lightbulb when my wife walked into the room and said, "You can't see a thing. I'll turn the light on for you." And she did, giving me an electric shock. FML

Today my five-year-old daughter watched me getting dressed in the bathroom and asked, "Mom, when my boobs grow, will they droop like yours?" FML

Today my mother bought me Mickey Mouse–shaped burgers for my dinner. I'm twenty-two. FML

Today my man and I were having sex on the edge of the bed. We were using chocolate spread, and I was riding him. When we were done, he got up and I noticed a long brown line on the edge of the bed. I knelt down to smell it. It wasn't chocolate. FML

Today my husband called me "my little zebra." I gave birth a month ago, and I've kept a few stretch marks. FML

Today the ugliest girl in school walked by me and said, "Ewwww." FML

Today a co-worker asked me if I had a comb he could borrow. I'm bald. FML

Today I went to Walmart with my mom.
I was eating a bag of chips in the
checkout line while my mom bought
her stuff. I inhaled while eating,
and I started to choke. The cashier
asked me if I was okay. My mom just
waved her hand and said, "Sometimes
she does that for attention. Ignore
her." FML

Today, while watching the trailer at the movies, my boyfriend elbowed me in the ribs and smiled during an ad for a weight loss institute. FML

Today my mom asked me for advice on how to give a good blow job. I'm a guy. FML

Today the guy I've secretly been in love with for years told me how hot my brother is. FML

Today I was lying in bed with my boyfriend, and he grabbed my double chin and went, "Gobble, gobble." FML

Today I figured I'd throw my ex-boyfriend a compliment and told him how "gifted" he was below the belt. He thought he was paying me a compliment in return when he told me how much he loves that little roll of skin that pops up over the top of my pants when I sit down. I'm trying to lose weight. FML

Today I have to be at work with a smile on my face while sitting next to the asshole who dumped me last week. FML

Today I'm looking for a job, and the employer I spoke to by phone was busy, but before hanging up he said, "We will call you soon." He never asked for my number. FML

Today I told my mom that I want to have liposuction. She said, "What's the point? You can't have lipo done on your face." FML

Today my boyfriend showed his mother
photos of me. She thought that I looked
like a celebrity from her country of
Korea. Flattered, I Googled this
celebrity. She is a porn star who's
had multiple cosmetic surgeries. FML

Today I sent my résumé to about a dozen jobs on Craigslist.
I realized that I hadn't updated it in a while, so I went to
double-check it after the fact. My ex had changed my objec-
tive to "I'm a cocksucker who needs a job real bad." FML

Today my dad walked into the arena where I was watching a
hockey game with my boyfriend and his friends. My dad was
wearing a crazy gray Mohawk wig. My boyfriend had just finished telling me how embarrassing it would be to be that guy's
kid. FML

Today I went to the doctor to talk about my depression and
low self-esteem. He told me that I shouldn't think of myself as
a fat pig for being overweight. I didn't think I was overweight.
FML

Today I asked my mom how much she had set aside for college. She looked at me as if I were crazy and said, "Why the hell would I do anything like that?" FML

Today I went out to eat with my aunt and uncle. I barely looked at the cute waiter because I'm a terribly shy person. Then my uncle exclaimed, "You should take out my niece! She's never dated in her life." I'm twenty-eight. FML

Today I handed in my PhD dissertation, which I have spent the past year researching and writing full-time. Last night, my roommate set an autocorrect in the word-processing program that changed "neither" to "nigger." I didn't notice until after I had handed it in. My professor is black. FML

Today my boyfriend asked me to go to a car show. I told him to hold on, I had to ask my mom. I quietly asked her to say no for me. She loudly said, "Sure!" FML

Today I was playing with three kids that I look after. The middle one has just learned about sex and, as a joke, started chanting that I had done it with the eldest kid. We were in the yard, and the neighbors heard. I was fired and escorted off the premises, and now I am being investigated by the police. FML

Today at work I was refilling some guy's iced tea, and the uppity jerk had the gall to ask me if I had ever kissed a girl, considering how fat I am, how high my voice is, and how little money I make. FML

Today I was complaining to my sister about how jealous I was of her looks. Her response was: "Sometimes it's okay to be the ugly sister. Like, you have less of a chance of getting raped." FML

Today I came to work with a new haircut, and everyone asked me if I had lost a bet. FML

Today I woke up next to a slumbering girl I had just met the night before. She had all the covers on top of her, and I was cold. Not only was *I* cold, but the sheets were really cold. When I got up, I realized that she'd peed all over my sheets. FML

Today I realized that it's been five days since my boyfriend last answered the phone when I called. Two weeks ago, he told me he used to break up with his girlfriends in a very juvenile way: He wouldn't answer their phone calls. FML

Today I told my girlfriend that I didn't feel wanted. Then she proceeded to talk about how her cat had puked on the carpet. FML

Today I was sitting at home, venting to my parents about how I never get asked out by any of the guys at school. My dad's words of wisdom were: "Don't worry, looks don't matter so much in college. Once they've had a few beers, they'll date anything." FML

Today I woke up to find that my dog
was missing. I had spent about an
hour searching for him, when my
psycho ex-girlfriend texted me his
photo. She'd kidnapped him. When I
drove over to her place, she shot
paintballs at my car. Now I have no
dog and a colorful car. FML

missbean

Today my girlfriend gave me a blow-up doll and told me to practice. FML

Today my wife left me the following voice mail: "Alex, last night was amazing. You took me to places I've never been to before. I can't wait to see you tonight after work." My name is Rob. We haven't had sex in two years. FML

Today I got a text message. It said, "I'm so drunk. What you up to, girl?" It was from my dad. FML

Today I went on a first date with a guy I had met at a speed-dating event. We went out to dinner, and he recommended the lamb shank, which I proceeded to order without looking at the menu. When the waiter took my order, my date said, "Wait, the lamb is $27, why don't you get the chicken." Then he ordered the lamb. FML

Today I sang at a retirement home with my school choir. Afterward, we went to speak to the old people, just to get to know them a little. The first woman I met asked, "Are you a boy or a girl?" FML

Today I texted my boyfriend to say hi. He responded, "I got your best friend pregnant." FML

Today my mother and I got into a huge fight about me being a lesbian. It ended with me saying "Fuck you!" to which she responded, "I bet you'd probably like to." FML

```
Today I wore a cute new striped
shirt to work. One of my co-workers
said to me, "I like your shirt. Most
fat people don't look good in
horizontals." FML
```

Today I heard my sister masturbating in her room. I took the dog around the block to get out of the house, and I came back to see her leaving her room...with my electric toothbrush in her hand. FML

Today I went to get my school picture taken. The photographer looked at me and said, "You look like you need a mirror." FML

Today I was tutoring kids at an elementary school. One kid messed up my hair. I said, "Why'd you do that?" He said, "I have lice. Now you have lice, too!" FML

Today my boss fired me via text message. I don't have a text-messaging plan. I paid twenty-five cents to get fired. FML

Today I got my boyfriend a pair of concert tickets for his birth-day. He loved the gift, but he turned to me and asked, "Do I have to bring you?" FML

Today I told my mom that I was going through a growth spurt. She said, "Yeah, horizontally." FML

Today I had to get my driver's license picture taken, and after the first try, the woman said, "It looks like your eyes are closed." I'm Asian. FML

Today we wrote Valentine's Day poems in class. I wrote a very depressing poem about how I had been rejected by all the girls I liked and how it hurt to be alone. When it was read to the class, they laughed and told me it was hilarious—even the teacher. FML

Today I went on a coffee date with a guy I'm interested in. He picked up his phone mid-date to finalize dinner plans with another girl. FML

Today I was trying on lingerie in the dressing room of Victoria's Secret, with my boyfriend next to me. I told him in a seductive, playful tone, "You can stay and watch if you give me a piece of your gum." He said, "Nope, I only have three more," and left. FML

Today, as I sat on my couch, heartbroken from a recent breakup, my mother walked up to me and in a very comforting voice said, "Maybe he left you for someone else." FML

Today I was at a fraternity party, and one of the hosts said over the loudspeaker, "Turn to the person next to you and picture them naked, then drink a beer if the mental image disturbs you." I turned, only to be face-to-face with my ex-boyfriend. He drank two beers. FML

Today I went alone to a fast-food restaurant to pick up food for a work party. I ordered 250 chicken fingers, 15 orders of fries, and 2 gallons of tea, and the guy behind the counter asked, "Is this for here or to go?" FML

Today I was sleeping, when my roommate walked in and asked, "So . . . when are you leaving?" She was throwing a party in our apartment. I wasn't invited. FML

Today my ex-boyfriend came over. After I finished pouring my heart out to him about how much I missed him and how much I loved him, he looked at me and asked, "So are we gonna do it or what?" FML

Today my boyfriend and I were hooking up while watching a movie. Just as I was really getting into it, he told me to move my head. He couldn't see the television. FML

Today I went to McDonald's for lunch and ordered a salad. The man behind the counter looked at me and said, "Well, at least you're trying." FML

Today I had sex with a guy for the first time. After he passionately made love to me, I turned to him and said, "You smell really good." He turned to me and said, "You don't." FML

Today I returned home from college and saw a framed picture of my parents and my younger sister on an elephant in the jungle. I pointed to the picture and asked my mom, "Is this some Photoshop job?" She responded, "No, we went to Thailand for a family trip. Didn't we tell you?" FML

Today I called my boyfriend, crying, to tell him I had the most terrible day. He said I should come over and he would make me feel better. I said that I just want to snuggle and that I was impressed with his sincerity. Then he said, "Can we snuggle . . . with my dick in you?" FML

Today I went to chill with my best guy friend and his girlfriend, whom I had recently met after I moved to the area. After a few beers, my buddy leaned over and tried to make out with me. I quickly backed up and, shocked, looked over at his girlfriend, expecting the same reaction. She winked. FML

Today at work I was reading *The Very Hungry Caterpillar* to a class of five-year-olds. I got near the end of the book and said, "Look at the big fat caterpillar," to which one of my pupils replied, "Just like you!" FML

Today I complimented my mom by saying, "Hey, I think you lost some weight." She replied, "Yeah, I think you found it." FML

Today I was feeling really upset and called my boyfriend. He said, "Can you feel upset a little later? I'm watching a movie." FML

Today my grandmother patched my
$300, vintage, limited-edition
designer jeans because she thought
I'd accidentally ripped them. FML

Today my mom decided to give me relationship advice. She told me that the key to a happy and successful relationship is "letting your man explore *all* your orifices." FML

Today I was playing basketball with my little brother. After I jokingly blocked his shot, he turned to me and said, "You're a bitch." He's six. I asked where he had heard that word, and he replied, "Daddy calls you that when you're not around." FML

Today my grandmother told me that not only does she not accept me as a homosexual man, but she feels my relationship with a little person is "spitting in God's face." FML

Today I met a guy at a bar, and we went back to my apartment. We started having sex, and about thirty seconds in, he stopped and said that it wasn't right, that he liked me too much for a one-night stand. He gave me his number and a kiss on the cheek and left. He had already come. I called his phone. Wrong number. FML

Today I made a couple of videos of me playing guitar and singing some of my favorite songs. I arrived back from school to find my family huddled around the camcorder, laughing, imitating me, and making jokes about the video. FML

Today my brother joked that our dog was more attractive than I was. I looked to my mom for support, and she said, "Well, she *is* a purebred." FML

Today I returned from a half-month-long trip to China with a group of friends. I threw myself into my mother's arms and burst into tears because I was so happy to be home. She stopped me to say, "Listen . . . these last couple of weeks have been some of the best I've ever had. Can we try to keep it like that?" FML

Today I woke up to the sound of scissors. My mom was cutting my hair while I was asleep. FML

Today I went to the doctor with my parents. When the doctor asked if I was sexually active, I said yes. My mom laughed and said, "Good one." My dad, for added effect, said, "Your hand doesn't count." FML

Today I saw my mom sneaking meat into her spaghetti sauce. She proceeded to tell me that she sneaks meat into most of the food she cooks. I've been a vegetarian for eight years. FML

Today I went to get a condom because my boyfriend and I were going to have sex for the first time. When I opened the drawer, I saw that every single condom had a Jesus pin stabbed through it. A note on top of the box read: "Love, Mom." FML

Today I kissed my girlfriend, and she tasted like a cigarette. I don't smoke. She doesn't smoke. My roommate does. FML

Today my boyfriend called me from a pay phone because he had lost his phone at the airport. When I texted his phone to get a response from the person who had it, I received a message back saying, "Love the pics. Send more ;)." FML

Today I was discussing sex with some of my guy friends, and I asked one of them what he would do if I got naked and got into his bed. He replied, "Nothing. You're one of the guys now." They all agreed. FML

Today I stopped at a lemonade stand on my way to work. A cute little girl handed me a mouthwash-sized cup of juice, and her adorable little brother told me it would be twenty-five cents. All I had was a $20 bill. He shoved it into his overalls pocket, looked up with huge brown eyes, and just said, "Thank you!" FML

Today I came home to tell my parents about the nose job I had done about a month ago. My mom always told me I should get one, so I didn't tell her about it right away, to see if she would notice. I was home for about twenty minutes before she asked me, "So when are you getting that nose job?" FML

Today I was at my ex-girlfriend's house. I still have a major crush on her. After cuddling, we watched a movie, and she began to show me several pictures of herself that she had taken on her cell, asking which ones I liked best. She then sent the pictures I had chosen to a guy she had met a week ago. FML

Today my friends and I were celebrating one friend's promotion.
Karen walked in and one of them
asked, "Karen, why aren't you drinking with us?" She replied, "'Cause I
would wake up tomorrow with you in
my bed and a lot of questions."
Karen is my mom. FML

Today I knew that my girlfriend was having a bad day. I went out to bring her frozen yogurt at work, because she loves it. When I was in the elevator, I overheard her colleague saying that the reason she was upset was because she had been cheating on her boyfriend with her new intern. FML

Today my sister asked if she could look through my closet to find something to wear. She is six months pregnant. FML

Today my boyfriend said that being with me was his payment for past sins. FML

Today I had a performance evaluation meeting with my boss. He told me I was the best in my department and that the productivity has never been higher since I started working here. He continued, saying that because everything is working so well, they don't need me as much, so he's cutting my hours. FML

Today an elderly gentleman walked into the UPS Store where I work, asking to use the laminating machine. I explained to him that we keep it behind the counter and that I would do it for him, at which point he produced several graphic photos of him having sex with nasty-looking women. FML

Today my girlfriend was packing for her study abroad program. As a joke, I had bought her a box of condoms. She laughed, saying, "Oh yeah, I'll definitely need some of those." Later, I showed up to take her to the airport and saw her open suitcase in the kitchen, with the condoms on top. FML

Today I wanted to have a nice lunch
with my wife before fasting for the
surgery I'm having tomorrow, which
I might not survive. She decided
that getting her hair cut was more
important. I ate alone. FML

Today I flew to New Zealand to surprise my girlfriend, who was on a trip. At the Auckland airport, I got a text message saying that she wanted to break up with me. I live in Michigan and had just spent $1,500 for this romantic surprise. FML

Today I found out that my mother has another new boyfriend. She told me she wanted me to meet him, and I reluctantly agreed. When I walked out to the living room to meet him, to my surprise, I already knew him. He's eighteen; my mother is forty-four. He also happens to be in my second-period math class. FML.

Today my family was leaving for a weekend trip and was supposed to pick me up on the way. About an hour before they were supposed to arrive, my mom called to tell me that there was no room left in the car so they wouldn't be stopping to get me. FML

Today my mom invited my girlfriend and me over to her place. Out of the blue, she pulled out my grandmother's wedding ring and gave it to me, saying that I could now propose. My girlfriend started screaming and said yes. I have been seeing someone else for three months and was planning to break up with my girlfriend. FML

Today I was over at a friend's place until very late. At some point, he stole my keys as a joke, but by the time I noticed, he was too drunk to remember where he'd hidden them. FML

Today at work a woman came up to the checkout counter, and when I greeted her, she said, "Oh, honey, you are so beautiful!" I immediately smiled and thanked her, but she looked at me and said, "Oh, not you," pointing to her ear. She was on her Bluetooth. FML

Today my dad woke me up at six, told me to take a shower, and drove me to school, only to say, "Just kidding. Happy snow day!" FML

Today I decided to be a good driver and not run through the yellow light. As soon as I stopped my car, another came and rear-ended me. The guy told me to pull into the parking lot so we could exchange information. As I drove into the parking lot, I turned my head and watched him drive away. FML

Today I was on my way home from a friend's house. I called home ahead of time to let my parents know I was coming. My dad picked up and in a panting voice said, "Now isn't a good time. Drive around the block for fifteen minutes." FML

Today I was talking to my mom. Out of the blue, she asked me, "Does he take his leg off when you guys are having sex?"—referring to the guy I've been seeing, who has a prosthetic leg. My dad then asked, "Does he beat you with it, too, if you've been naughty?" FML

Today my girlfriend and I were being driven home from our date by her mother. My girlfriend is Jewish, and I'm Catholic. Her mother was talking about how my girlfriend was going on a trip to Jerusalem that summer. She finished by saying, "And you can find a nice Jewish boy while you're there." FML

Today the fitting room of the store I work in smelled really bad. The customers started to complain, and since I was on fitting-room duty, I went to investigate. A middle-aged woman had pooped on the floor and put a chair on top to cover it. FML

Today I received a card in the mail. It was from my vet's office. Inside the card they had written: "We send our sympathy during this trying time." I haven't been home in three days. I can't find my dog, and my mother won't talk about it. My dog was seven. She hated that dog. FML

Today I flew home early from a two-month trip to Europe to surprise my boyfriend on his birthday. When I got to his house with a cake I had baked from scratch and a quilt made with silk-screened pictures from my trip, his roommate answered the door and said, "Oh, sorry, he's out with his girlfriend." FML

Today I was teasing my little brother. Later that night, I went to the bathroom to wash up. While brushing my teeth, my little brother slipped a photo under the door that showed him scrubbing my toothbrush against his nuts. FML

Today my boyfriend and I went out to eat. The waiter came to take our order. My boyfriend said he wanted a cheeseburger. I ordered the same. My boyfriend looked at me and said, "Are you sure you don't want a salad?" FML

Today someone stole my phone at a concert. They thought it would be funny to text my mother that I was pregnant. FML

Today my mom decided to give me a solid reason for not having premarital sex. She told me that my future husband will want me to be tight for our first time. My mom and I were on a ski lift. The ride lasted ten more uncomfortable minutes. FML

Today my mother and I went to Walmart to buy sanitary pads. I suggested that I get tampons instead, so that I can go swimming at my boyfriend's cottage. My mother then went up to the nearest store employee and said, "Excuse me, if my daughter uses a tampon, does that mean she is no longer a virgin?" FML

Today my white mother-in-law called our house phone. Since I'm Chilean and have a fairly heavy accent, she mistook me for the cleaning lady and scolded me for answering the phone. Before I could correct her, she said, "This is why only white people should be allowed in America" and hung up. FML

Today my mother told me that she needed a urine sample from me to send to the doctor to test for allergies. I did what she asked and went to my room. I came downstairs later and found her in the bathroom putting my pee on a pregnancy test stick. FML

Today I had drunken sex with a girl I barely know. I didn't have a condom and was nervous about getting her pregnant, but she assured me that I could pull out. Just as I was about to pull out, she wrapped her legs around me and yelled, "BE MY BABY'S DADDY!" I couldn't get out in time. FML

Today I was in my backyard scolding my cat. I yelled, "If you can't learn to use the bathroom correctly, then I am going to leave your stupid butt out here in the snow until you figure it out!" Later, my neighbor left me a nasty note about child abuse. FML

```
Today I was at work, and a very
obese woman came in to get a pedi-
cure. When she took her shoes off, I
noticed an odd black substance on
her feet. I started scrubbing it off
and wondered out loud, "What is this
stuff?" As a chunk of it fell onto
my lip, she replied, "Girl, that's
just the fungus." FML
```

Today my roommate got mad at me for putting away the tampons that had been sitting on her desk. She rebelled by hanging hundreds of tampons, dyed red, from every surface in our room. I discovered this while giving my mom her first tour of the place. FML

Today my boyfriend and I were about to have sex. Just as things were heating up, my closet door flew open and my little brother ran out screaming, "Mom, they're doing it, come quick!" My mom had paid my nine-year-old brother to spy on me. FML

Today I had just finished having dinner with my boyfriend, so I leaned over to him and said seductively, "How about some dessert?" He looked at me and said, "Babe, you really don't need it." FML

Today I took a cab home from the airport. The taxi driver was on the phone and not really paying attention. I paid him and got out of the cab, but he drove away before I could get my luggage out of the trunk. FML

Today I decided to tell my mom about my choice to wait to have sex until after marriage. Coming from a very Christian family, I thought she would be proud. Instead, she laughed and said, "Is that your excuse for not being able to get laid?" and walked out of the room. FML

Today I asked my parents whether the outfit I was wearing made me look fat. My mom looked at me and paused for a while. My dad said, "Honey, that outfit doesn't make you look fat. Your fat makes you look fat." FML

Today I turned twenty-two without anyone wishing me a happy birthday. In fact, the only phone call I received all day was from my brother. He wanted to borrow money. FML

Today my mother finally had her beloved Siamese cat cremated. The cat had been dead for over a week, and she had been keeping it on her bed, stroking its fur and saying, "She looks like she's sleeping" and "She's so cold." To top it all off, she's been calling me by the cat's name for three years. FML

Today, as I was bagging groceries at
the supermarket, I looked down to
see a six-year-old urinating on my
shoes and on the floor next to me. I
told his mother that she should take
her kid to the restroom, only to be
told to "mind your own goddamned
business." I was later fired for
arguing with a customer. FML

missbean

Today my Christian boyfriend of six months broke up with me. I had told him when we started dating that I was an atheist, and he just now decided to look up what that means. He gave me a Bible. FML

Today I had one of the worst panic attacks I'd had in years. I was worried that nobody cared about me and that I had completely messed up my life. I was hyperventilating and crying hysterically. My mom walked by my room, looked at me, and said, "If you're going to make those noises, at least shut the door." FML

Today my girlfriend dumped me for someone else. An hour earlier I had gotten permission from her dad to propose. FML

Today I was swimming in the ocean with my best friend, and a giant wave came and knocked off the bottom of my bikini. My friend told me that she would go get another pair of bottoms so I could walk onto the very crowded beach. She left me there for half an hour, laughing from the shore with her entire family. FML

Today, while I was lying in bed with my girlfriend, she was grabbing the fat on my stomach. I told to her to stop touching my fat. She replied, "So don't touch you at all?" FML

Today I jokingly had a sexual conversation via text message with a good guy friend. He was pretending to be a stranger and was fishing for compliments and asked to have a foursome. It turned out that my friend had lost his phone and I had spent two hours talking to a random pervert about the lingerie I was wearing. FML

Now it's your turn. Write your own FMLs.

Today ....

....

....

....

....

.... FML

.....

Today ....

....

....

....

.... FML

Today ....

....

....

....

....

.... **FML**

• • • • •

Today ....

....

....

....

....

.... **FML**

Today ....

....

....

....

....

.... FML

. . . . .

Today ....

....

....

....

....

.... FML

Today..
....
....
....
....
....
.... FML

•••••

Today..
....
....
....
....
....
.... FML

274

Today ....
....
....
....
....
....
.... **FML**

· · · · ·

Today ....
....
....
....
....
.... **FML**

Today ....

....

....

....

....

.... FML

• • • • •

Today ....

....

....

....

....

.... FML

Acknowledgments

Our thanks go to:

Julien Azarian, Alan Holding, Frans van Schoor, Marielle Bonnard, Isabelle Abraldes, Camille Bourély, and Laura Cherfi, for their everyday involvement in the F My Life adventure.

About the Authors

MAXIME VALETTE was born on April 30, 1988, in Reims, France, the area where champagne is produced. There has hardly been a time in his life when he hasn't had a computer keyboard at his fingertips. He began programming when he was nine years old and creating websites at eleven. He started a business at fifteen and sold it at eighteen to found Beta&Cie, through which he created the VDM website (the French version of FML). Besides computers, his hobbies are music, TV, and wine.

GUILLAUME PASSAGLIA was born on January 28, 1982, somewhere on the Côte d'Azur. He likes polar bears and enjoys vodka martinis (shaken, not stirred). He is an IT engineer, part-time photographer, and keen sportsman. He is also an unfaltering Internet games fanatic, but is now involved in another kind of game—directing several international companies. He is also in charge of the spotlessness of the studio apartment where the VDM and FML team meets to plot out the future. He likes perfection, and his ultimate goal is to one day beat Didier Guedj at tennis.

DIDIER GUEDJ was born in Paris many years ago. After studying international business and landing a job in marketing, he quickly realized that he'd be better off working as a full-time musician. He began by creating jingles for advertising campaigns. He then became creative director of several ad agencies, before finally founding his own agency. Overseeing brands such as Heineken and Dunlop, as well as several French perfume manufacturers and bestselling books, he has been the brains behind more than a hundred ad campaigns. He claims to be the devil.

About the Illustrator

MARIE "MISSBEAN" LEVESQUE was born on September 6, 1982, in Paris, France. After graduating from high school and spending three years training to become an architect, she is now a full-time illustrator. She lives and works in a small one-room apartment in Paris, but plans on moving soon into a castle in the south of France. Marie likes beer and chocolate, and she spends her spare time taking close-up photos of insects, as well as watching movies while asleep, which is the main reason that she can never remember the end of any of them.